HOW TO MAKE MONEY WITH STOCK OPTIONS

a Basic Guide for the Conservative Investor

MERVYN L. HECHT

VANTAGE PRESS
NEW YORK

SECOND EDITION

Copyright © 1999 by Mervyn L. Hecht

Published by Vantage Press, Inc.
516 West 34th Street, New York, New York 10001

Printed in Hong Kong
ISBN: 0-9662481-1-2

Library of Congress Catalog Card No: 91-91497

0 9 8 7 6 5 4 3 2 1

*Dedicated to Naim and the Colonel,
who helped me learn; and with thanks to
my friends Sybil Fields, Ray Swartz, and
my wife Dr. Bonnie Hecht who helped
me write what I learned into English.
Also with thanks to Dr. Russell Taussig,
who contributed both text and
ideas to this edition, and Jean Ross
who helped with editing.*

CONTENTS

List of Figures

HOW TO MAKE MONEY
WITH
STOCK OPTIONS

Preface

About 15 to 20 years ago one of my tennis buddies decided to become a stock broker. He and I had been comparing notes on the market for some time, and occasionally one or the other of us had engaged in various option strategies or short selling. Options were very new then, and there were very few stocks against which options could be written.

A few weeks after he took it up on a full time basis, he showed up at my office with a computer terminal. He proceeded to show me how the computer terminal was able to accept selection parameters, and then print out any available options that met those parameters. For example, if I wanted to sell CALLS against stocks for a minimum return of 15%, the computer terminal would scan all of the available options, do all the mathematical calculations for me, and let me know if any such covered writing positions were available in the market on that day.

This opened my eyes to a whole new world of investing, and from that day on I was hooked on options.

I was not the only one. Another friend of ours became so excited about option writing that he rented an office right in the stock brokerage firm and spent every morning there for many years writing options on a daily basis. Many times he and I would sit together and work out new strategies to follow.

A short time later, I became active in the formation of an investment advisory company that specialized in writing options for clients. During that process I learned some very interesting points about our society. I learned that many – if not most – large institutions were hiring invest-ment advisors with option writing experience so as to increase the return on their portfolio. For example, the investment advisors handling the funds for major univer-sities had become very active in option writing.

But there were few or no investment advisors writing options for individuals with modest stock portfolios. Option writing seemed to be the prerogative of the super rich.

One of the reasons for this was, and has continued to be, the perception of options in the individual segment of the investment community. When I once suggested to my mom that she let her broker write some CALLS against her stock positions, to increase her income, she was hor-rified and looked at me as if my birth must have been one of the major aberrations in her life. I never mentioned it again.

But the aversion that mom and her friends have for option writing has a certain justification In our society. When I practiced law, many client cases came to me where investors with portfolios of more that $100,000 but less than $5,000,000 had lost large sums of money by allowing their brokers to buy or sell options in their account. In almost every case the losses arose from the fact that the broker had thought he understood options, but really did not, and this lack of understanding had put the client at vastly more risk than the client was prepared to accept.

And yet, it has always been clear to me that option writing can be done on a very conservative basis, with limited and defined risks that can be adequately understood by the individual investor, and communicated by a broker to a client. Friends that have asked me about option writing, and heard me make that statement, are usually intrigued by it and want to understand it better. Unfortunately, cocktail parties – where these conversations often take place – are usually too short for an adequate explanation of option writing. So, at the request of several friends, I began to look around for a book which I could recommend to them to explain what kind of strategies I was engaged in, and what conservative strategies they could follow.

I was disappointed in my search. I found lots of interesting books on how to make money in buying real estate, how to make money in selling real estate, how to make money in buying options on real estate, and not really buying it, and how to make money in selling options on real estate and not really selling it. I found books on how to make money by investing in stamps and gold coins, and a number of other things, including macadamia nuts and iguanas. But I did not find any books that explained, in simple language, how to make money in stock options. I did find a few very excellent books that explained stock options and stock option strategies. The disclosure document put out by the Chicago Board of Options Exchange itself, which is sent to all investors in options through the Exchange, is pretty good. There are some much more detailed and voluminous works which cover virtually every element of option writing, and which can serve as excellent resource books. Lately, some books have become available which cover very sophisticated strategies for using computers to help devise option strategies and plays which I find very exciting. But all of these books are too long, too detailed, and too voluminous for me to give to my friends. My friend Jeff, the dermatologist, claims that he is not willing to devote more than three hours to reading anything about an investment. If it takes more time than that, he claims, the nature of the investment is too complex for a medical doctor.

I think he is right. I don't think an investor has to understand all of the complexities and intricacies of the options market in order to include options trading as a part of his or her normal investment strategies. Average investors in the stock market can master two or three conservative, fixed-risk option strategies and use them comfortably in their investment programs.

And so I wrote this book (mainly to protect myself at cocktail parties). My hope is that I have written in simple enough language so that the average investor in the stock market, with a medium sized portfolio, can understand some of what I have said. It is not necessary to understand everything I have said. It is only necessary that in reading through the book, one or two strategies are understood. The investor can then try these strategies once or twice, and with the help of a stockbroker with adequate training, engage in those strategies which are appropriate and of interest.

No doubt there will be those who claim that this book is still too hard to understand. I once heard that a student of the great philosopher Immanuel Kant criticized Professor Kant for writing books that were too complicated for human understanding. To this Professor Kant replied: "If you can make these ideas that simple, you will indeed become a famous man."

It is unlikely that I – or anyone else – will become famous by simplifying the language of option strategies. But I might help someone begin to better understand how to handle options, and that's all I'm trying to do.

The reader must accept the fact that some of the ideas are in fact complex and require reflection and experience to fully understand. But that is true of the stock market itself. An investor who just buys stock without understanding the fundamentals of the company and the economy is risking whatever he pays for the stock. To understand all of the fundamentals of the company and the economy is a potentially infinite task to which many brilliant people devote their lives. Of course, no investor expects to fully understand the fundamentals of the company, and certainly not of our economy, which are constantly changing. We are satisfied with looking at certain financial information about the company, and various "indicators" about the economy. Fortunately, the option strategies discussed in this book are not as complicated as the overall financial data of a large company, nor are they as complicated as an understanding of the principles of economics. The principles of option writing can be reduced to certain rules that every investor can understand. Some will understand them after reading about them once, and some will need a little more time to study and think about them, depending on the reader's level of sophistication and experience in investments.

Because I believe that these principles can be understood by an investor of moderate sophistication, I was willing to undertake the effort to write this book.

Los Angeles, California

January 15, 1992

Mervyn L. Hecht

Preface to Second Edition

I began buying and selling stock options in the 1970's, even before the Chicago Board of Options Exchange opened. At that time most people had little interest in options, except a desire to know what they were. After a while interest picked up, and a few funds used options for hedging, or for premium income. But those funds were not popular with the public, and didn't stay in business. A few years ago when I was looking for a mutual fund that used options for premium income, in which to invest my own money, I couldn't find one.

Then during the mid-1980's some of the larger investors became more interested in options. Private funds began to look for managers that were knowledge-able in options. A few books came out on the subject. But by and large my belief is that most of the option activity was done by very sophisticated investors, controlling large blocks of money.

During the crash of 1987 a lot of investors, brokers, and stock brokerage firms with option investments were badly hurt. Some were hurt because they didn't know what they were doing, and were in a position of great risk, which materialized. Others knew what they were doing, but didn't think such a drop could occur so suddenly. This latter group knew the risk, but considered it to be only a theoretical risk. There were a lot of lawsuits brought, and many, many arbitrations. As is so often the case, when faced with massive criticism resulting from options transactions, brokerage firms tightened up their rules, and in many cases put severe restrictions on the brokers and investors wanting to do option writing.

Much of this generalized fear of options persists today. But within the past year or so I've begun to sense a difference in climate. There is more interest in using options (as well as other derivatives). Most importantly, there is a growing understanding of the wide range of uses to which options can be put. The Nobel prize in economics was recently given to two men for their work in the valuations of options. Many new books are coming out on options. The options markets are increasing in volume. Options are becoming almost "mainstream" in the world of investment.

What I still sense in the world of options is a general misunderstanding by the non-professional investor of those uses of options which limit risk. There certainly are a fair number of non-professional investors using options, especially as a means to increase income from premiums. But the more sophisticated uses of options which enable the investor to profit from the increase or decrease of a stock or index price, profit from the lack of volatility of a stock price or index, or protect a holding against declining value, are not understood by most investors.

Nor is there much literature designed for the non-professional investor.   The books on options that I've reviewed during the past year are not written for the non-professional investor, and many would be difficult reading even for the most experienced professional.

While option strategies are not for everyone, I believe that most investors can master the basic concepts, and use them to advantage.   Above all I believe that an investor who understands and uses options can invest with less risk than one who doesn't use options. And that is the fundamental reason for this book.

July, 1998

Port Grimaud, France

PART I - Introduction

Current Attitudes Toward Stock Options

Stock options have a bad name. Many investors refuse to have anything to do with them, having heard that they are "speculative." For example, in some lawsuits, judges and jurors take it for granted that if a stockbroker or investment advisor engaged in stock option transactions for an investor, it was automatically a "speculative" investment.

In the following pages I hope to convince you that many stock option strategies are not speculative, and are less risky than the purchase and sale of stocks. The one difference is that stock option strategies are more difficult to understand, and it takes more time to learn the vocabulary. For this reason, part of this book deals with understanding the vocabulary of stock options.

But this is not really a book about options. It is a book about risks in the options market. There are already a

number of books that explain options, generally in much
more detail than options explained in this book. The
Chicago Board Options Exchange (CBOE) pamphlet on
options, which is routinely sent to investors who trade in
options, contains a lot of valuable information on options
and examples of various option strategies.

There are now several mutual funds that advertise that
they buy and sell options to achieve a higher yield for their
investors - and for some investors, letting the experts
handle these kinds of trades is the best decision.

As a result of this literature, lots of people know and
understand the basic principles of options.

Yet, in the 25 years that I have been involved in option
trading, I have been amazed at the lack of general understanding of what is a "risky" strategy, and what is not, of
what is "speculative" and what is not. Many people -
some of whom surely should know better - think that any
option trade is inherently speculative. At the other
extreme, I have known experienced brokers using risky
strategies they sincerely believed (and told customers)
could not lose money!

The truth lies somewhere in between. Some strategies
are high risk, and some are low risk. Some are speculative and some are conservative. Some are appropriate
for the particular investor, and many are inappropriate.

The purpose of this book is to try to define these terms, and to identify some of the more common strategies that fall into each group.

As a consequence, this book is not thorough in its discussions of the principles of options. It is written primarily for people who either know something about stocks, and want to learn more about options.

Part one is a summary of option history, principles and risks. Part two is a compilation and discussion of basic option strategies. Parts three - five describe some of the more common complex option strategies including those that should be classified as "conservative." In each part I try to identify what the risk is, and why.

In this way, I hope to play a small part in clearing up the widespread misunderstanding of the relationship between risk and option trading.

A. The Differences Between Options and Stocks

Owning a stock is not the same as owning a house. When you own a house you can live in it, you can fix it up, and you can see it every day. Many people think that the same is true when they hold a stock certificate in their hand. They can see it and feel it, it has an attractive gold or green border, and it is made of fine quality paper. (See Figure I-1.)

Mervyn L. Hecht

Figure I-1 Stock and Option Certificates.

a stock certificate

[does not exist]

an option certificate

But the fact is that the stock certificate itself is merely representative of a group of intangible rights that the holder may or may not be entitled to exercise. If your name appears in the right place on the stock certificate, and also appears in the right place in the company records, and if the company has managed to stay out of any kind of bankruptcy proceeding, and if certain other facts have remained constant, then you may have the right to vote at a shareholders meeting, the right to exchange voting rights under certain situations, the right to receive dividends, and the right to sell the certificate.

Some or all of these rights can be taken away from you by action of the board of directors of the company, or by your creditors, or by creditors of the company. Whatever rights you have you can probably exercise whether or not you have the certificate, as long as your name is properly inscribed on the shareholder register of the company. For that reason, and for convenience, many, if not most, shareholders never take possession of stock certificates in companies in which they own stock, but allow the stock certificates to remain in "street name" with their stock broker. This means that the company lists the brokerage house as the owner, and the brokerage house lists you as the owner. These shareholders have the same rights as do shareholders that hold a certificate, but instead of certificates they have the right to instruct the stockbrokerage company to do the same things that a stockholder with a certificate can do in person.

Buying or selling a stock option gives the buyer or seller certain rights which are very much the same kind of rights as a stockholder has. As explained below, the buyer of a CALL has a right to buy a stock at a certain price under certain circumstances. Obviously the right to buy something at a fixed price is not the same as already owning it, but it is not very different in terms of the potential for profit.

In any event, when thinking about options it is important to realize that we are talking about the same kinds of intangible rights that the holder of a stock certificate has. Some people believe that this "trading in rights" is a new, weird "end of the century" phenomenon. But option rights in and of themselves are not so new. The first option transactions arose from transactions in ancient Egypt. By the time of tulip trading in Holland in the 1600's they were quite popular in the commercial community.

The kind of options that we deal with today arose from commercial contract transactions of the type with which we are all familiar. Suppose that a vineyard owner is in the process of growing ten acres of grapes. He knows that if he can sell the grapes for $1,000 per acre, when the grapes are mature, that $10,000 in gross receipts will be adequate for him to pay all his expenses and live comfortably until the next harvest. (Not only is this story apocryphal but grapes are usually sold by volume not by acre).

He also knows that while grape prices may be slightly higher than $1,000 per acre at the moment, they are subject to fluctuation, depending on quality and availability at harvest time, and that he may therefore eventually get more or less than $1,000 per acre. Meanwhile, at the wine production facility, the wine producer knows that if he can buy grapes at $1,000 per acre, he can bottle the wine, sell it at a reasonable price, and make a fair profit. He too knows that grape prices may fluctuate, so there is a possibility that he may have to pay substantially more than $1,000 per acre, and thus not make a profit for the year.

It behooves these two entrepreneurs to meet together, and agree in advance to buy and sell future production for $1,000 per acre. Note that such a "future" sale is reminiscent of the old story of the fellow that sold the Brooklyn Bridge - the farmer is selling something that he doesn't (yet) own. The wine producer acquires a right to buy something in the future which does not yet exist.

A slight modification of the contract between these two people would create an option transaction. If the owner of the vineyard sells the right to buy the grapes to the wine producer for $1,000 an acre, but the producer is not obligated to buy, the producer has acquired a CALL option. It is the decoupling of the right to buy from the duty to sell that creates the option.

And so, you may ask, under what circumstances would

the owner of the vineyard be willing to give the wine producer the right to buy, without requiring him to have the
duty to buy. As is so often the case in life, the answer is
that the vineyard owner would only do that if he were paid
sufficient money to make it worth his while. Suppose, for
example, that the vineyard owner is reasonably certain
that the price of grapes will never fall below $900 per
acre. Yet, at $900 an acre he will not make enough prof-
it to live comfortably until the next harvest. Suppose further that the wine producer is willing to pay $100 per acre
for the rights to acquire the production for a further payment of $900 per acre. Since at a total cost of $1,000 per
acre he can make a reasonable profit, the producer now
buys a "CALL option." He pays $100 for the right to buy
the production for an additional $900 per acre. The vine-
yard owner has "hedged," so that his risk of not having a
successful year is extremely small. The producer has
paid $100 per acre to create a reasonable certainty of a
profitable year.   Each side has protected himself form
economic disaster for the year, at a small price relative to
the overall transaction. If grapes are selling below $900
per acre at the end of the year the option will not be exercised, and the vineyard owner will get the current price of
grapes plus the $100 per acre he received for the option.
He is $100 per acre better off than he would have been.
The producer still can make a nice profit, but less than if
he hadn't bought the option. If the price is over $1,000
per acre the vineyard owner only gets $1,000 per acre
($900 plus the $100 option price) and the wine producer
has purchased grapes at $1,000 per acre. In this case,

the vineyard owner made a reasonable profit, but gave up and lost an extraordinary profit. The extraordinary profit was, in effect, passed to the producer.

Through the use of the option, both the seller and the buyer made their business transactions more conservative.

It is this ability to create protection and to collect a premium that permits options to be utilized by the conservative investor to create conservative investment strategies.

B. The Hard Part Is The Vocabulary

Because options deal with (1) the underlying security, (2) a strike price, (3) a premium, and (4) a limited time, and because they are often traded in groups (combinations) that are described with special names, the vocabulary of options becomes important. So we start there.

ALWAYS REMEMBER, HOWEVER, THAT THE OPTION IS A BUNDLE OF RIGHTS IN AND OF ITSELF - NOT AN APPENDAGE TO THE UNDERLYING STOCK. THINK OF AN OPTION AS IF IT WERE REPRESENTED BY ITS OWN "CERTIFICATE," WHICH FLUCTUATES IN PRICE LIKE STOCK CERTIFICATES DO.

C. Understanding The Terminology: 11 Key Terms

The following discussion is very basic and certainly not thorough. More complete discussions of option writing are available in many publications, including the pamphlet distributed by the Chicago Board of Options Exchange to everyone who opens an options account with a member firm. Brokers also have access to materials in their company's procedure manuals. The following brief summary is all one needs to understand options. It is presented in accordance with my personal views of what the important concepts of option writing are, and how they should be conceptualized. Reading definitions is no fun, but a basic understanding of the vocabulary is essential to further understanding of the concepts.

I classify options into four categories: stock CALLS, stock PUTS, index CALLS, and index PUTS. Some texts on options that I've seen properly define PUTS and CALLS and then assume that a PUT and a CALL on an index fits the same definition. Because I think that the risks and strategies involved in PUTS and CALLS on stocks are very different than those on indices, I recommend thinking about these four kinds of options as if they were four different pieces of paper, like stock certificates, each representing a different kind of investment.

When talking about an option, the option should be designated by the underlying security, its termination month, its strike price, and its type. For example - one "Ford Jan 35 CALL" - is an option to buy 100 shares of Ford Motor Co. At $35 per share until the end of the third trading Friday next January. (See Figure I-2.) With that basic information in mind, here is a brief definition of the eleven basic option concepts for repeated reference:

1. CALL. One stock CALL is a right to buy 100 shares of stock at a particular price until a specified time. We saw the CALL in action with our friend the wine producer. He bought a CALL to be sure he could acquire his grapes at a maximum of $1,000 per acre.

If I own one Ford January 35 CALL, I have the right to buy 100 shares of Ford Motor stock at $35 per share through the close of the business day of the third Friday of that January. Alternatively I can sell the CALL itself. If I own such a CALL, someone sold it to me. That person has committed to sell 100 shares of Ford stock to me if I exercise my option. If I exercise my option, the stock is said to be "called away" from the seller. Note that the seller might already own Ford stock and have sold a CALL against it, or the seller, if called, may have to go into the open market and buy the stock to "cover" the position.
There is no certificate issued to represent the option. It is merely an entry on your broker's books. Only the "confirm" you receive from your broker, and your broker's credit, guarantee you the option rights.

2. PUT. One stock PUT is a right to sell 100 shares of

Figure I-2 An Option listing from the Wall Street Journal

Option & N.Y. Close	Strike Price	Calls-Last Oct. Nov. Jan	Puts-Last Oct. Nov. Jan
FORD			
32	35	1/8 1/4 5/8	3-1/4 r 4-1/4

This listing is one line of the options on the Ford Motor Company. The day preceeding this listing, Ford stock closed at $32 per share. The strike price illustrated is $35 per share. Other horizontal lines show different strike prices and relative option prices.

CALL options with a strike price of $35 for October last traded at 1/8. This means that a Ford October 35 CALL would cost 100 times 1/8 or $12.50 plus commission. The November Ford 35 CALL option last traded at 1/4 and the January at 5/8ths.

Note that the November PUT is not priced, it is restricted.

stock at a particular price until a specified time. In our wine story, this would exist if the grower paid the producer $100 per acre for the <u>right to sell</u> the producer the grapes produced for $1,100 per acre. The grower has protected himself from a price decline below $1,000 per acre, and the producer has collected $100 per acre in exchange for the contingent promise to purchase at a price he can afford to pay.

Similarly, if I own one Ford January 35 PUT, I have a right to sell 100 shares of Ford Motor stock at $35 per share at any time through the expiration date. The person that sold the PUT to me has become obligated to buy the stock. As with the CALL, I can also sell the PUT itself at any time during its life. (See Figure I-2.) I may already own the 100 shares, and have bought the PUT to protect its value. Alternatively, if I do not own the stock and if the stock price goes down during the option period, it will pay me to purchase the stock and then "put it" (sell the stock because of the PUT) to the buyer at the higher ($35) price. The result of the transaction will be that I sold high, then bought low, which never hurts!

3. INDEX CALL. The S&P 100 index is described below. For the moment it is sufficient to understand that an index CALL gives the holder the right to collect a varying sum of money until a specific time, as the index rises above a specific number. For example, if I buy one index CALL at $300, and the index goes up to $310 before the CALL expires, I instruct my broker to exercise the CALL and my broker will put $1,000, less transaction costs, into my account. Alternatively, if the index goes to $290, nothing happens: I bought the CALL, and paid my premium to the seller who took the risk. Since the index did not go up, I just lose the premium that I paid for owning the option. Because it is an index, I do not in fact buy or sell the actual stocks that make up the index. I am only dealing in money.

4. INDEX PUT. An index PUT gives the holder the right to collect a varying sum of money, until a specified time, as the index falls below a specific number. Thus, if I buy an index 300 PUT, and the index goes up, I lose my premium. If the index goes down, I make $100 for each point it went down upon exercise or expiration. I can exercise my option at any time until it expires. If I wish, I can "close out" the position before it expires. If I own the position I can sell it at the market price, and if I have sold the position I can "buy it back" at market price at any time, unless market liquidity is affected by special events, as happened during the crash of 1987.

5. STRIKE PRICE. We have talked about the "strike price" in the previous examples. The "strike price" is either the dollar value of the stock, or the number of the index, specified in the option. Thus, in the examples above, when we talked about a Ford 35 CALL the strike price is $35. When we talked about an index option at 300, the strike price is $300.

6. TERMINATION DATE. The "termination date" is the

date on which, at the close of business, the option rights expire unless exercised. Most options expire at the end of the third Friday of the designated month. Note that you can exercise an option (or be put or called, if you are the seller) at any time during the life of the option - not only at the end of the period. Also note that you must initiate some action through your broker, or else the option may expire worthless even if it still has value!

7. AT-THE-MONEY. An option is "at-the-money" when the actual present dollar value or index number is the same as the strike price specified in the option. The option is "in-the-money" when the stock or index price goes past the strike price in the direction of profit for the holder: and the option is "out-of-the-money" when the current price is not yet at the strike price, in the direction of the loss for the holder. (These terms are illustrated in Figure I-3.)

8. COMBINATION. A "combination" is a strategy where more than one set of related option rights is held at the same time. A "spread" is a particular type of combination. In addition to spreads, perhaps the most common combination for option traders is to buy or sell an out-of-the-money CALL and out-of-the-money PUT on the same security at the same time. This combination is described in greater detail below.

9. TIME VALUE PREMIUM. "Time value premium" is the market value of the option excluding "intrinsic value."

FIGURE I-3 At-the-Money, In-the-Money, and Out-of-the-Money CALLS and PUTS on a $20 Stock.

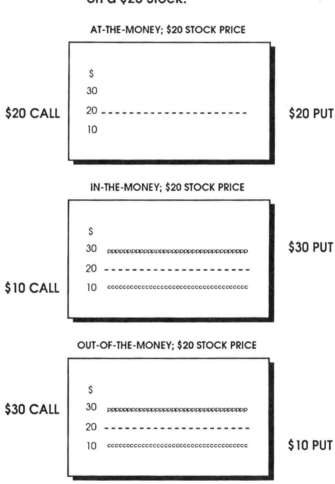

(Time Value Premium is illustrated in Figure I-4.) Time value premium is what the conservative option seller is trying to capture.

10. INTRINSIC VALUE. "Intrinsic value" is the amount of money, excluding "time value premium," which could be realized from an option at a specific point in time. (This is illustrated in Figure I-5.)

11. LONG AND SHORT. We speak of a holding as "long" when we own the position. To own a position means that you have purchased it, whether voluntarily or involuntarily. Accordingly, of you buy a CALL you are long that CALL. If you sell a CALL, you are short that position. If I say "I am long the Ford 55's and short the Ford 50's," that means that I bought the Ford CALLS with a strike price of $55, and sold Ford CALLS with a strike price of 50. I would then have to specify the termination date to fully describe my position. If I also own the Ford stock, I can be described as "long Ford." If I own 1,000 shares I might describe it as "long 1,000 shares of Ford."

D. Basic Examples

Now that I have listed the definitions of the key option terms for your reference, let us look at some examples. In these examples, I will alternatively use the pronouns "he" and "she" in describing the parties to the transaction , but there is no particular significance to either pronoun.

Mervyn L. Hecht

FIGURE I-4 **"Time Value Premium" (T.V.P.) for an Out-of-the Money CALL with a Strike Price of $30.**

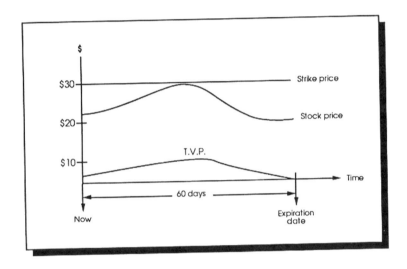

The Time Value Premium goes up as the price of the stock gets closer to the strike price ($30), but declines with time.

(1) The Stock CALL Purchase

The best known option is the stock CALL. One stock CALL gives the holder (the buyer) the right to buy 100 shares of the stock. For example, if IBM is $100 per share on December 15, you can expect to buy a January 105 IBM CALL for approximately $2. If you buy that CALL, since each CALL represents 100 shares, you will pay approximately $200 (plus between $25 and $50 in commission) and for that premium you will receive the right to buy 100 shares of IBM stock for $105 per share until the close of the business day of the third Friday in January.

Since the stock has not yet reached $105, the $2 that you are paying is strictly "on the come." Unless the stock goes over $105 a share, your option will expire worthless. The option is therefore "out-of-the-money." The strike price of the option would have to be below 100 in order for the option to be "in-the-money." Since most options trade in multiples of $5 or $10, the $95 strike price is the closest one that is "in-the-money." The 100 option would be "at-the-money."

Why would anyone buy a January 105 CALL on IBM? The buyer of that option may believe that there is a substantial likelihood that IBM stock will go over $107 by the expiration date. Note that the stock has to go over $107 for the buyer to make any money. If the stock only goes to $106, the buyer can buy the stock for $105, and imme-

FIGURE I-5 Intrinsic Value and Time Value Premium Components of the Price of an In-the-Money CALL Option.

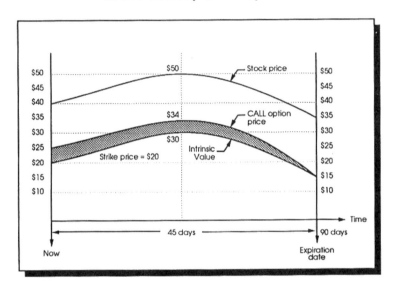

TODAY	IN 45 DAYS	IN 90 DAYS
INTRINSIC VALUE 20 (40–20)	INTRINSIC VALUE 30 (50–20)	INTRINSIC VALUE 15 (35–20)
T.V.P. = $5	T.V.P. = $4	T.V.P. = $0
TOTAL PRICE $25	TOTAL PRICE $34	TOTAL PRICE $15

The Time Value Premium shrinks with time, while the Intrinsic Value changes with the stock price. If the option were not so far In-the-money, the Time Value Premium would fluctuate more as the stock price approached the option strike price.

diately sell it for $106, gaining a $1 per share advantage, or $100, but since the buyer paid $200 for the option, at $106 the buyer still loses $100. [For simplicity I am eliminating transaction costs such as commissions in these examples, except where they become significant to the discussion.]

The buyer of an option like this has a somewhat different mind-set than the buyer of IBM stock. The buyer of the stock has a substantial sum of money to invest, in this case, 100 shares at $100 would be $10,000. Presumably the buyer of the stock is willing to invest that sum of money because he believes that the stock will rise in value at some time in the future, coupled with the potential for dividend income. The option buyer in this example is not willing to invest $10,000. Because the option buyer believes that he or she can predict the rise of the stock within a specified time period, and the prediction can be tested for a small amount of money (the cost of the option), the buyer is willing to risk $200.

As you will learn below, however, it is likely that this option buyer has purchased the option as part of a more complex strategy, either to capture some portion of a premium, or to hedge a different position.

(2) The Stock CALL Sale

Now, let us look at the other side of that transaction, from the perspective of the person who sold the CALL that the buyer purchased. Perhaps at that moment IBM stock is not much in favor with the investment counselors and stock market pundits. The company has had disappointing earnings, and sales are not as strong as expected. Some say the whole computer industry is weakening. Competition by Compaq and Apple is strengthening. The seller doubts that IBM stock will reach $105 in the near future. He is therefore willing to sell one or more CALLS of IBM and collect $200 per CALL, less commissions. If, between mid-December and the end of next January, approximately 30 days, IBM stock does not go over $105, the seller of the CALL will keep the $200. If IBM goes over $105, the seller will be "called" and will have to sell the stock at $105 per share to the owner of the call, or buy new stock at the market price to deliver to the owner of the call. If IBM goes over $107 the seller will lose $100 for each point that the stock exceeds $107 when the option is called. Note that the seller might be "called" before the expiration date, if IBM stock goes over $105 at any time before the expiration.

Why would a "CALL writer" make this sale? Perhaps it is greed. Greed is a strong driving force in the stock market. The prospect of collecting an easy $200 is attractive. If you make that sale without adequate information about IBM stock, you are speculating. The speculation carries with it a theoretically infinite risk, since theoretically the stock could go up to any number. But, as a practical matter, even if you have no information about the stock, a Blue Chip stock like IBM, is unlikely to go up say, 50% in a 30 day period. So, while there is a theoretically unlimited risk, even if it cannot be precisely defined, there is some practical limitation. And, of course, the risk can be contained by various strategies, such as owning the underlying stock.

NOTE THAT THERE IS AN IMPORTANT DIFFERENCE BETWEEN THE BUYER OF THE CALL AND THE SELLER OF THE CALL. THE BUYER OF THE CALL RISKS ONLY THE PRICE OF THE OPTION. THE SELLER OF THE CALL RUNS A RISK WHICH IS NOT PRECISELY DEFINED.

(3) Stock Indexes

Options on a stock index are very different than stock options. Indexes on commodities or interest rate futures are again something very different. To understand options on a stock index, it helps to first understand what a stock index is.

Many stock index options are written on an index referred to as the "OEX," the proper name of which is the "Standard & Poor 100 Index." This is also commonly known as the "S&P 100." Be careful not to confuse it with the "S&P 500," which is a more frequently quoted index.

The S&P 100 is a group of 100 allegedly market representative stocks selected by the Standard & Poor Company. In the old days the index that everyone heard about was the Dow Jones Industrial Average, based on 30 allegedly representative stocks widely quoted by news commentators. (See Figure 1-6). The S&P 100, which I will refer to in this book as the OEX, fluctuates, generally speaking, in parallel fashion with the Dow Jones Index. Because of the way the index is constructed, as a rule of thumb the Dow Jones Index moves 7 or 8 points for each 1 point of the OEX. So on a day when the news reporters say that the Dow Jones went up 22 points, I would expect the OEX to have moved up between 3 and 4 points. As I write this, the Dow Jones is fluctuating around 3000, and the OEX is at approximately 360, so the ratio of the total is not 1:8, but the fluctuation is, roughly speaking.

The OEX is important to us in this discussion because it is the index on which most index options are written. But there is a big difference between writing an option on an index and writing an option on a stock. If you buy an IBM Jan 105 Call before the option expiration date, you might take delivery of 100 shares of IBM stock for $105 a share. If you buy an OEX Jan 330 CALL, you can't take delivery. If you exercise your option, which you would only do if the OEX goes over $330, all you get is money. This is a very big difference which is of particular importance when we compare the sale of a PUT against a stock to the sale of an index PUT. So, first, let us look at the purchase and sale of a stock PUT, and then come back to compare it with an index PUT.

Figure 1-6 Stocks Making up the
Dow Jones Industrial Average

The Dow Jones Industrial Average is the oldest continuing measurement of the U.S. stock market. The index is a price-weighted index of 30 of the largest, most liquid stocks listed on the New York Stock Exchange. Trading in options began on Monday, October 6, 1997.

Index Components as of February 11, 1999:

AA	Aluminum Company of America	3.39%	ALD	Allied Signal Inc.	1.99%
AXP	American Express Co	4.49%	BA	Boeing Co	1.72%
CAT	Caterpillar Inc.	2.31%	C	Citigroup Inc.	2.24%
CHV	Chevron Corp	3.71%	DD	Du Pont Ei De Nemours	2.54%
DIS	Walt Disney Co	1.33%	EK	Eastman Kodak Co	3.39%
GE	General Electric Co	4.09%	GM	General Motors Corp	3.15%
GT	Goodyear Tire And Rubber Co	2.61%	HWP	Hewlett Packard Co	2.88%
IBM	International Business Mach	7.59%	IP	International Paper Co	2.02%
JNJ	Johnson & Johnson	3.70%	JPM	JP MOrgan And Co Inc.	4.95%
KO	Coca Cola Co	3.16%	MCD	McDonalds Corp	3.21%
MMM	Minnesota Mining	3.69%	MO	Philip Morris Co	2.57%
MRK	Merck And Comp	6.70%	PG	Procter And Gamble	4.10%
S	Sears Roebuck	1.96%	T	AT And T Corp	2.88%
UK	Union Carbide Co	2.01%	UTX	United Technologies	4.69%
WMT	Wal Mart Stores	3.13%	XON	Exxon Corp	3.27%

Underlying Level: Both near-term & leaps are based on 1/100th of DJIA Level.
Multiplier: $100
Expiration Months: Up to three near-term months plus up to three months on a quarterly cycle. Leaps w/exps.
          up to 3 years in future.
Strike Prices: Set to bracket index level in 1 point increments.
Option premium quotes: One point = $100
Exercise: European-style
Settlement: Cash–based on opening prices of stocks Friday of expiration
Last Trading Day: Thursday before expiration
Trading Hours: 9:30 A.M. to 4:15 P.M. Eastern time
Exchange: Chicago Board Options Exchange
Symbols: DJX
Final Settlement Value Symbol: DJS
Divisors: 25.133811 (11/20/97)

Leap Symbols:	WDJ	December 1998	
	VDJ	December 1999	VDK (Eff. May 11, 1998)
	LDJ	December 2000	LDK (Eff. May 11, 1998)

(4) Stock PUTS

If I buy an IBM Jan 100 PUT when IBM stock is at $100, I can sell 100 shares of IBM, until the expiration of the PUT, at $100 per share. Obviously, if IBM goes down below $100 per share, it will pay me to sell it for $100, and buy it back at the open market at the lower price. If IBM stock goes down to $95 during my option period, I can sell 100 shares at $100 by exercising my PUT option, buy 100 shares at $95 on the open market, and make a $500 profit before commission.

Assuming that I paid $2 per share for the PUT, or $200 total, that is the maximum amount I can lose. I will lose the $200 PUT option price if the stock stays at $100 or goes over $100. Why would I do that?

If, after adequate research, I felt fairly certain that IBM stock will go down significantly within the next 30 days, for a small amount of money (the cost of the PUT option), I will be able to profit from the decline. This profit would be greater, in relation to my cost, than if I were to sell the stock short.

Since for every buyer there is a seller, let us examine the seller's state of mind. The seller has concluded that either IBM is not likely to go below 100 during the next 30 days, or if it does it's a good buy at that price. If the seller is engaging in this transaction as an isolated transaction, the seller's motive in making the sale is either to collect the premium, or to acquire the stock during a dip in price.

Again, while it is possible that the buyer or the seller is engaged in this transaction as an isolated transaction, it is probably part of some broader strategy, such as those discussed below.

(5) Index PUTS

The sale of an index PUT is very different from the sale of a stock PUT. The seller of an IBM 100 PUT has assumed the risk of being obligated to buy IBM stock at $100 per share. This seller may well believe that the purchase of IBM stock at $100 a share is a good investment for the future even if the stock does not go up in a short term. By collecting a $200 premium, this seller is really only committing to purchase IBM stock at a net price of $98 per share, the $100 price that it is put to him or her, less the $2 per share already received as a premium. If the investor would be willing to buy 100 shares of IBM stock for $98 per share anyway, there is virtually no additional risk in selling this PUT.

But the seller of a PUT on the OEX cannot take possession of the underlying stocks. Consider the sale of 1 OEX PUT Jan 330. For each point that the OEX goes below $330 the investor has a potential loss, if put at that time, of $100 per point. A single day 100 point drop in the Dow Jones, or 12 or 15 point drop in the OEX, is no longer uncommon. Therefore a $1,500 loss is easily within the realm of possibilities. Many would say that taking the possibility of a $1,500, or even perhaps a $3,000 loss to collect a $200 premium is a risky, speculative investment. We will examine this at greater length in later discussions in this book.

The purchase of an index PUT is more like the purchase of a stock PUT, but where the stock price can fluctuate from activities affecting that company, the index is less susceptible to such changes because of the leveling effect of the stock basket on which the index price is based.

(6) Index CALLS

The buyer or seller of an index CALL may or may not be in a different position from the buyer or seller of a stock CALL. Let's look at the case where the investor has a large diversified portfolio, containing all or many of the same stocks which make up the S&P 100 Index. If that investor sells an out-of-the-money CALL on the index, the risk factor is not very different from an investor with holdings in IBM who sells a CALL against the IBM holding. The most significant difference is that the investor with the specific stock, IBM in our example, may be required to deliver the stock if the price of the stock goes above the strike price. If the seller of the CALL sold the CALL in the hopes that the stock would be called away at the strike price, the investor selling the CALL against her stock portfolio accomplished a sale of the stock. This does not happen with the seller of an index CALL. The seller of the CALL cannot deliver the underlying stocks at expiration. But, if the investor has a number of stocks that have gone up in value, those stocks can be sold to pay for the loss from the sale of the CALL. So in this sense there may not be much difference.

One significant difference, however, is that the seller of a stock CALL is subject to any unusual increase in that particular stock. For example, if that particular stock suddenly becomes the target of a takeover offer, the stock can jump way up in value. This can be very costly to the CALL seller. This is less likely to happen on an index CALL, since it is comprised of many different stocks. From this point of view, the seller of the index CALL is in a more conservative position than the seller of a CALL on a particular stock if he does not own the underlying stock.

E. What is "Speculation"?

What do we really mean when we say that an investment is "risky" or "speculative?"

From one point of view all stock investments are risky and speculative. There have been massive frauds in some of the finest blue-chip companies which caused the stock to drop like a bomb. Do you remember the missing oil in the American Express tanks? Or the phony insurance policies at Equity Funding?

Some stocks are riskier than others. Some of the new emerging bio-technology stocks seem unlikely to produce a profit unless and until they develop a product to sell. On the other hand, steel companies seem to have trouble finding buyers for their product.

The textbook definition of "risk" centers on "volatility." Stocks on companies perceived as volatile are deemed more risky than others. The problem with that traditional definition is that the nature of the companies changes all the time, at least in the world as it is today. In an earlier edition of this book IBM was used as an example of a non-volatile stock. At that time the stock was selling at approximately $160 per share. Soon after the book came out the stock dropped to about $60 a share. Later the stock started back up, split two for one, and at the time of this writing is over $100 per share, or the equivalent of $200 per share for the pre-split stock. The stock certainly seems volatile, but is an investment in IBM "risky?"

As in many areas of life, it seems that the term "risky" is a matter of gray, not black and white. Stock ownership in general is perceived as less risky than option transactions because of the impermanence of options. Stocks that pay dividends can be considered a safer asset to hold, because the dividend acts as a hedge against inflation, and a bottom point for the decline of stock price (based on yield).

After quality dividend paying stocks, in order of increasing riskiness, comes non-dividend stocks. Owning these stocks, which have an unlimited time to increase in value, seems less risky than options, which have a limited life and decline in time value premium as the length of their life shortens.

But if this is true, what can we say about a short option position? As time passes, the premium shrinks, and the likelihood of a profit to the investor-seller increases! Is an option sale therefore less risky than owning stock?

Suppose IBM stock is $120 per share today, and, based upon lots of data, you draw two conclusions: first, that the stock is likely to go up, and second, the worst case decline over the next 90 days is 20 points, bringing the price of the stock down to $100 - a 16% decline.

-If I buy 100 shares at $120, I pay $12,000 and my assumed "worst case" risk is $2,000.

-If I buy one 90 day CALL at 120, perhaps I pay $400. My investment is $400 and my maximum loss is $400.

-If I sell one 90 day PUT at 120, I might collect in $400. My assumed "worst case" risk is $1,600 (a 20 point drop at $100 per point, less the $400 premium).

So the greatest potential dollar loss in this example is the outright stock purchase, and the lowest is the purchase of the CALL. From one point of view, the stock purchase is the most risky.

So which strategy is the most risky? I don't know. It is a problem of definition, and point of view.

The point is that "risky" is not a very useful term for describing a market strategy. It is too broad and too general. What is important is to KNOW YOUR RISK. Option investors get into trouble when they engage in strategies not fully understood by them. That results in unexpected loss.

Let me give you an example:

Mrs. Krinsky had bought lots of stocks throughout the years. Then her broker told her about options. "A wonderful thing" he explained. "You go short 10 PUTS and collect $1,000 immediate profit with low risk. All you need is $10,000 in back-up money."

The broker was correct. He was selling way-out-of-the-money PUTS on a blue chip stock, and the risk of the stock declining, based on an historical analysis, was very small. Mrs. Krinsky, with a net worth of several hundred thousand dollars, thought of the transaction as a purchase for $10,000. If everything went wrong (not likely) she might lose her $10,000 "risk" money. But for $1,000 profit every 60 or 90 days that seemed reasonable. But the unlikely risk materialized. The stock dropped to a new 20 year low. There was a $25,000 loss. Mrs. Krinsky was shocked. She understood the concept of risk. What she did not understand was the EXTENT OF THE RISK.

This misunderstanding led to an unpleasant lawsuit.

Maybe "speculative" means something different to investors than "risky." We all take risks (driving on the Los Angeles freeways, for example) and the concept of risk is endemic in the concept of investment. But none of us has to "speculate."

Yet the term "speculate" must mean something important. I note that several brokerage houses list "speculative" as one of the investment goal choices in the customer application form, sometimes automatically applied to uncovered option writing.

Do many customers invest with a goal to "speculate?" I doubt it. I think the brokerage house legal counsel put that choice there for their own protection, so option writers who later complain can be shrugged off as "speculators." Yet I have seen some option trades that one can only describe as speculative: close-to-the-money combinations on relatively volatile stock, written repeatedly for premium income, where anyone should have expected an eventual big negative hit, wiping out all the premium income and then some.

In the long run, I suspect that the term "speculative" is just used to identify trades that the user of the term believes subject the investor to a high likelihood of loss. But the term is not used carefully, and the usage has therefore carried over to whole categories. Because of the lack of precision in this usage, this term, like "risky," is also not very useful. For these reasons, I suggest avoiding these terms altogether, and talking instead about the "appropriateness" of a trade or position for a particular investor. In addition to avoiding the looseness of the other terms, the term "appropriate" takes into consideration the financial position of the investor, psychological considerations, broker expertise, and risk-reward relationships -concepts usually not considered in a "risk" or "speculative" analysis.

I do not use the term "suitability," although it is close in meaning, because it carries with it certain legal connotations which may not be synonymous with good judgment. Some strategies which are suitable under the law are used with poor judgment, and are not appropriate.

In this book, then, I speak of the appropriateness of various strategies and trades for various investors. When I refer to a "conservative strategy," I mean one which is appropriate to a conservative investor. By "conservative investor" I mean one who is primarily interested in conserving capital, in an inflation prone economy, and earning reasonable income with very low risk of capital erosion. That is the person (directly or through his or her advisor) to whom this book is addressed.

When I refer to the "conservative investor," it is necessary to also consider another characteristic. Anyone who tries to make money in the stock market by predicting the likelihood of a short term rise and fall in stock prices, gold prices, or interest rates, is speculating. While I have the utmost respect for many researchers and economists, I have never seen any statistics which show a correlation between intelligence and the ability to predict the stock market, or between educational background in the field of economics and the ability to predict the future of interest rates.

Absent such statistics I have come to the conclusion that the MOST conservative way to trade options is to take "neutral" positions which do not depend for profitability upon a prediction of a future price change. The best way to do this is by capturing option premiums through the sale of options. Capturing option premiums really puts the investor into a position not unlike the position of an insurance company. Nobody thinks that insurance companies are risky, and everyone considers the insurance industry very conservative. Thus, an investor that can be like an insurance company, and take a certain amount of controlled risk in exchange for which people will pay premiums, will be a conservative investor.

And so, when referring to option strategies for conservative investors, one important strategy is selling hedged options for premium income. Certain strategies discussed in this book are strategies appropriate for conservative investors, since they are designed to capture option premiums in positions where the risk is controlled. To better understand this concept, let us compare the relative positions of the buyer and the seller of an IBM 100 CALL to see if we can understand which one is taking the greater risk.

Clearly both parties to the transaction, buyer and seller, are speculating if they have not carefully investigated the appropriate financial data about IBM. Buying or selling any financial investment without knowing quite a bit about it (or relying on trustworthy information from a knowledgeable party) is a gamble. So, let us assume that both parties are knowledgeable about the prospects of IBM, but that reasonable investors could hold varying opinions as to what the stock will do within the next 30 days.

Since option rights lose time value each day until they expire, the buyer has paid a premium for an asset that decreases in value each day that the expiration date draws nearer, unless the stock price goes up over the strike price. (See Figure 1-7).

The seller, meanwhile, has collected a premium that can be invested in something else, including an interest bearing security, during the option period. The buyer is relying on his or her ability to predict a stock price fluctuation in order to make a profit. The seller is in a more neutral position; she needs only to hold the opinion and rely on lack of volatility of the stock price in order for the trade to be worthwhile.

One might say that the option buyer is engaged in a

FIGURE I-7   Erosion of Time Value Premium Over Time.

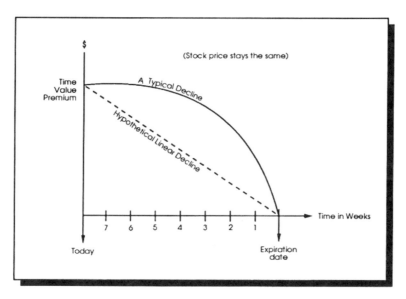

WEEKS TO EXPIRATION	HYPOTHETICAL	TYPICAL
8 =	1.0	1.0
7 =	0.87	0.93
6 =	0.75	0.85
5 =	0.62	0.79
4 =	0.5	0.71
3 =	0.375	0.61
2 =	0.25	0.50
1 =	0.12	0.36
0 =	0	0

more risky transaction than the buyer of the underlying stock itself because of the short time period obtained through the option. But looking at it from a different point of view, one could say that because of the large investment required to buy the stock, the buyer of the stock is risking more money, and is more likely to lose because of the loss of the use of the funds for a long period of time during which the stock is held.

From another point of view, whether or not the option buyer is "speculating" depends on (1) the relative amount of money spent by the buyer to acquire the option, compared to the buyer's total investment portfolio; and (2) whether or not the information obtained by the buyer was reasonably sufficient to conclude that the stock was likely to go up an appropriate amount before the expiration date. In other words, if the buyer acted reasonably, the trade is reasonable, and if the buyer acted unreasonably, the buyer is speculating just like the buyer who buys a stock with inadequate knowledge.

Now, let us look at the question of speculation from the seller's point of view.

The seller is typically thought to have engaged in a high risk transaction because of the theoretically unlimited risk incurred. As already explained, the risk is not really unlimited. There is some dollar figure which everyone could agree is beyond the realm of any reasonable likelihood for the stock to go to. No one would think it possible for IBM stock to go from $100 to $300 in a 30 day period. There are, of course, recent examples of takeovers where stock has gone up 20-40% in a matter of weeks. Some stocks have a much higher intrinsic value, realized on liquidation of the company's assets, than is reflected in the price of the stock in the open market. But that theoretical "takeover price" can be computed. So, again, I believe that whether or not the seller of this CALL engaged in a risky trade depends on the information available to the seller in determining the likelihood of the stock going up more than an expected amount in the following 30 day period. Additionally, the seller's ability to absorb loss is an important factor.

There is one more element which should be considered concerning risk in this transaction. For the seller the cost to hedge against a large loss is relatively small. To hedge the sale of a 100 CALL, if the stock is, say, $95, one can buy a CALL 10 or 15 points above the strike price of the short position (here, over 100 - say the 110 or 115) for a relatively small premium, and thereby be in a clearly defined risk position. This "spread" strategy is explained further in this book.

From a conservative investment point of view - and clearly from a litigation point of view, - it is very difficult to justify the failure of a seller to hedge such a short position, particularly if it can be done for a reasonably small price.

What can we say in conclusion? Any investment, if not

well thought out and researched, should be considered risky and is inappropriate. Investments which can result in a loss beyond the financial resources of the investor's risk capital are inappropriate for that investor. Using options as an investment resource can reduce the risk of many investments. Some option strategies are conservative in nature, and can produce or enhance income with little risk. It is those strategies to which this book is devoted.

F. How to Enter and Order

All exchange traded options are settled through the Options Clearing Corporation, sometimes called the "OCC." This clearing house, comprising well capitalized brokers, guarantees each option transaction. Once an option trade has been settled on the floor of any exchange, the parties no longer look to each other for delivery and payment, but look to the OCC. Thus, the OCC becomes the buyer to every seller and the seller to every buyer.

Every purchase of an option contract from someone is offset by a sale by someone else. But all transactions go through the OCC, which acts as a middleman for the transaction, and thus removes the credit risk inherent in the old "over-the-counter" market. There is also more liquidity, since a market maker is required to buy all options offered for sale.

A market maker is a person who quotes a bid and ask price for an option whenever asked to do so. The "bid" is the buy price, and the "ask" is the sell price. Market makers do not handle public orders; they buy and sell for their own accounts only.

A customer wishing to buy or sell options must contact a broker, who relays the order to a floor broker for execution. The floor broker deals with the market maker. An order book official, known as a "board broker," keeps a record of unfilled limit orders, that is, an order to buy or sell at a specified price (the "limit") or better. Information on all outstanding limit orders is available to all traders. This system is in contrast to the system of specialists who make a market in particular stocks, and who also keep the book, but do not reveal that information to other traders. The CBOE claims that the use of board brokers leads to more efficient trading. Not every option exchange uses the board broker system.

There are two kinds of orders in general use with options. The most common is the "**market order**," a simple order to buy or sell an option at the best possible price as soon as the order gets to the exchange floor. While this is the most simple and most common, I do not recommend it. I recommend a "**limit order**," an order to buy or sell at a specified price or better. I decide in advance what price I am willing to buy or sell at. I tell the broker that price. If the order goes through, good. If not, the broker calls me back and tells me why, and what the current price is.

Some traders use a "**good till canceled**" order. This means that the order remains in effect until it is specifically canceled. I suggest against this kind of order. Options are too volatile, and the memory too short, to have an order outstanding for an infinite period of time. I recommend, at the most, placing an order that is good until the close of the business day. Then you can look at it again the next day and decided if you want to put it on again or not.

Finally, when entering an option trade with more than one position included, such as a spread, it is advisable to include an instruction of "**all or none**," which means that all the positions, or none of them, should be executed. Along the same lines, when entering an order for a spread or combination it is best to specify a combined net credit or debit. For example, if trying to buy a call at $2, and selling a put at $1, put in the order "all or none for a net debit of not over $1."

PART II - Basic Strategies

A. Buying an Option [NOT recommended]

Obviously, the most simple option strategy is just to buy an option.   You can buy either a PUT or a CALL. Whichever you buy, your risk is limited to the amount that you pay. When you buy an option, your only risk is that you will lose the premium that you paid. If you pay very little for it, and you have reasonable grounds to believe that you might make a profit, it seems to be a reasonable investment, and not very "risky." I think some people confuse "risky" with "wasteful." There is a certain element to the puritan ethic which considers it wasteful to buy something impermanent. Thus, it seems to some to be a waste of money to spend it on food or entertainment. But buying a sturdy piece of furniture would not be wasteful.

And so it is, to some, with buying an option. If you save up your money and buy a share of stock instead, you have something of permanence.   But if you buy the option, it expires.

If I use the work "risky" in this book, "wasteful" is not what I mean. By risky I mean that you are put in a position where there is a significant likelihood of losing an inappropriate sum of money. Therefore, buying an option, by my definition, is rarely risky. It may be stupid. It may be wasteful. It may be inappropriate. But it's rarely risky, because you know the cost at the outset, and that is what you can lose.

In my opinion, however, buying an option is usually only worthwhile if it is part of a larger strategy, such as a hedge against accepting too much risk. You will see examples of this when we discuss spreads below. To buy an option by itself and make money on it requires a correct judgment about a stock price change in a short period of time. Except where you have special information about a company, I have usually not found this to be successful, especially after transaction costs.

B. Selling an Option

The next simplest strategy is to sell an option. But this is quite a bit more complicated than buying an option.

First of all, when you sell an option there is a big difference between selling an in-the-money option and an out-of-the-money option. Selling an in-the-money option subjects you to much higher risk than selling an out-of-the-money option. And selling a long-term option usually brings in a much higher premium than selling a short-term option. But selling any option, in and of itself, generally subjects you to a very substantial market risk. For this reason, there are very few cases where it would be appropriate for an investor to just sell a PUT or a CALL, except where the sale is part of a larger strategy. Absent the ability to absorb the worst case risk, and absent extremely unusual and dependable information, this is the one area of options which is most likely to be inappropriate for most investors.

Why does the sale of an in-the-money CALL put the seller at greater market risk than the sale of an out-of-the-money CALL? Take a look at Figure II-1. The seller of the out-of-the-money CALL has a "window" of stock price volatility before the risk of loss materializes -i.e., the price increases to the strike price. But the seller of the in-the-money CALL is subjected to loss point-for-point with a rise in the stock price.

Because the sale of an in-the-money CALL can produce a large cash premium (the intrinsic value), one sometimes sees brokers selling them to cover up losses. The cash premium inflates the cash position in the account, although if the option is "priced" on the statement it reduces the account value. But in-the-money options usually have a lower time value premium component, and are therefore less valuable as a way to collect premium income.

As far as I know, there is rarely a valid reason for you

**FIGURE II-1   Comparing Risk of Sale of an
In-the-Money CALL with an
Out-of-the-Money CALL**

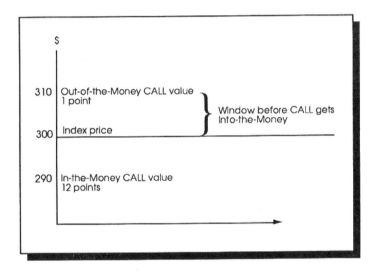

Within 10 points (the intrinsic value portion) the In-the-Money CALL will fluctuate almost directly with the market, because most of its value is intrinsic — that is, the difference between the index price (300) and the strike price (290).

The Out-of-the-Money CALL has no intrinsic value, and the seller is not at risk unless the indeX goes over 310. There is therefore a 10 point window of price movement before the risk of loss materializes.

One point is worth $100 per option.

yourself, or you on behalf of someone to whom you owe a fiduciary duty, to sell an uncovered option solely in the expectation of making a profit from that single position. That is because there is, in every case that I can think of, a way to hedge the risk for a nominal sum, without interfering with the primary motive of potentially profiting from the sale of the option. Since there is always some combination strategy which will work almost as well as the individual option sale, it seems to me generally inappropriate to engage in the simple sale of an option - except in one situation - the uncovered PUT. (See p. 61).

One appropriate use of the option sale is the sale of an in-the-money CALL to hedge a long in-the-money PUT position.

For example - when IBM stock is $100, I sell a $95 PUT for $3 (yielding a total of $300 less commissions) in an attempt to buy 100 shares of stock at $92 net per share if IBM dips below $95. I expect to be put the stock, that is, to be forced to buy the stock at $95 if the stock price falls below $90 during the option period. If the price stays above $95 I will keep the premium.

If the stock drops to $91 and stalls, I can sell an in-the-money CALL at 85 for $10 and collect $1,000. (Call prices become inflated when the stock becomes volatile - this $1,000 in premium consists of $600 of intrinsic value and $400 of premium value - See Figure I-5). If the stock price stays at 91 until expiration, I will acquire the stock at

FIGURE II-2   Use of an In-the-Money CALL as a Hedge for an Out-of-the Money PUT That Went In-the-Money

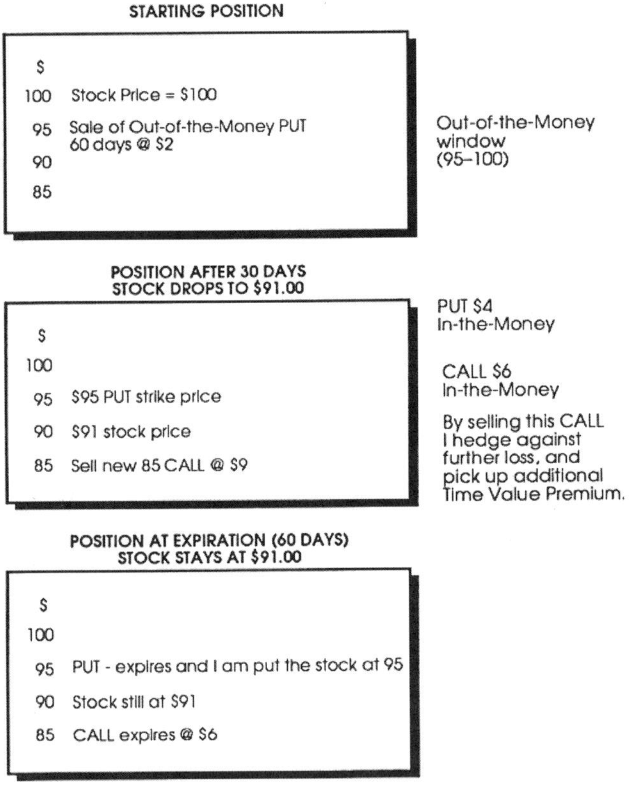

STARTING POSITION

$		
100	Stock Price = $100	
95	Sale of Out-of-the-Money PUT 60 days @ $2	Out-of-the-Money window (95–100)
90		
85		

POSITION AFTER 30 DAYS
STOCK DROPS TO $91.00

PUT $4
In-the-Money

$		
100		CALL $6 In-the-Money
95	$95 PUT strike price	
90	$91 stock price	By selling this CALL I hedge against further loss, and pick up additional Time Value Premium.
85	Sell new 85 CALL @ $9	

POSITION AT EXPIRATION (60 DAYS)
STOCK STAYS AT $91.00

$	
100	
95	PUT - expires and I am put the stock at 95
90	Stock still at $91
85	CALL expires @ $6

By selling the CALL I picked up $3 of Time Value Premium. Added to the $2 received on the original sale of the PUT, I have received $500 in premium. I own the stock at $95, and the stock is worth $91 — so I could sell out and approximately break even on the transaction. While the goal was not to break even, that's not a bad result for a stock that fell 9% in 60 days!

$95 per share. I collected $300 from the original PUT, and, after paying out $600 (91 less 85), the Call will make another $400 profit for a net stock price of $88 ($95 less $700 net in premium). I converted a prospective $100 loss on my original PUT position (95 less 91 was a $400 loss less the $300 collected in premiums) to a $300 profit: I was hoping to acquire the 100 shares of stock for a net $9,100 and in fact acquired it for $8,800.

At the same time the call acted as a hedge. The hedge feature works as follows:

If the stock price moves up after my sale of the CALL, I will lose $100 per point on the CALL, but make $100 per point on the put, which is now in-the-money (up to $95).

If the stock price continues to deteriorate, which is the risk I am hedging against by selling the in-the-money CALL, I will continue to gain $1 per point on the CALL down to $85. By selling the CALL I stopped my downside risk between a drop in the stock price from $91 to $85. If the stock continues to fall below $85, I can sell another in-the-money CALL and repeat the process. (See Figure II-2).

The calculation looks like this:

Premiums Received:

FIGURE II-3   Selling a PUT as a Method of Acquiring Stock.

STARTING POSITION

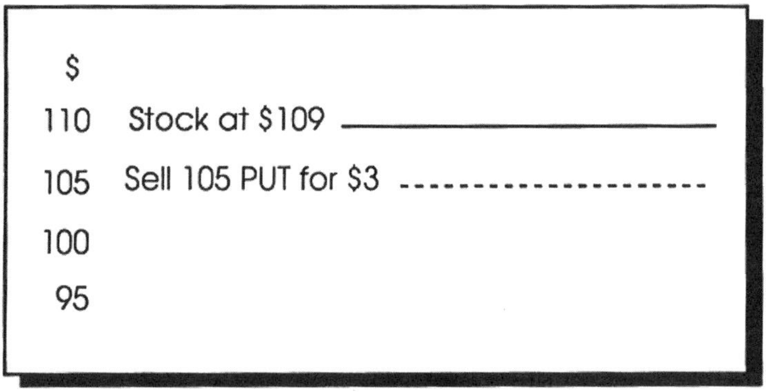

$
110   Stock at $109 ————————————————
105   Sell 105 PUT for $3 -
100
 95

AT EXPIRATION:

If the stock stays at $109, I keep $300 PUT premium and write another PUT. If stock is below $105 (for example $104) I will be PUT the stock at $105 less the $3 premium received for a net cost of $102 per share. That means that I am obligated to buy 100 shares of the stock, for a net cost of $10,200,

Sale of PUT	$ 300
Sale of CALL	+ 1,000
Total premiums received	1,300
Buying back the call	− 600
Net premiums received	$700
Cost of stock	− 9,500
NET COST	$8,800

I started out hoping to pay $9.200 for 100 shares of IBM stock if it dipped below $95. By selling a "rich" CALL, I improved my position by $400 at a low risk.

Under proper circumstances, selling an uncovered PUT is more conservative than buying and holding stock.

Suppose, for example, that I would be willing (and am financially able) to buy 100 shares of IBM at $102. But the stock is now at $109. At 109 I don't dislike it, but I don't love it. At $102 I like it, and I want it. At $100 I love it. So I sell the 105 PUTS at, say, 3 points (or I sell the 110 PUTS at say, 10 points if I really want the stock.) This means I agree to buy the stock at the strike price (105 or 110) at any time during the option period, because my net cost, with the premium I receive, is a price I am willing to pay. At expiration, if the stock has remained above my strike price, I rewrite, and I keep rewriting until either (1) the stock dips to my strike price, and I acquire it, (2) it rises beyond the point where there is any significant premium in the 105 PUT (or maybe I roll up to a higher strike

FIGURE II-4 The Buy-Write Strategy.

STARTING POSITION

$
120

110 Sell 10 CALLS @ 110 for $2

100 Buy 1,000 shares @ $100

90

At Expiration —

If stock is over $110:

Called away for:	$110,000
Cost was:	100,000
Profit of:	10,000
Plus premium:	2,000
TOTAL PROFIT :	$12,000

*PLUS ANY DIVIDENDS
BEFORE THE STOCK
WAS CALLED AWAY.*

If stock is under $110:

*Received $2,000 premium
and dividends.*

price), or (3) I've made so much premium writing these PUTS that I retire from the market. (See Figure II-3)

Any of these alternatives is not bad. The only negative is that if IBM moves up to $250 and never dips, I will kick myself for having written PUTS instead of buying the stock. But my billfold, swollen from profits from PUT premiums, will shelter the blow!

Writing PUTS in situations where the investor is willing and able to take delivery of the underlying stock is a sound conservative strategy. The main caveat is to be sure you have enough money on hand to buy the stock if that is the result of the strategy.

C. The Buy-Write [Strongly recommended]

One of the most common institutional options trades is the buy-write. In this trade, the investor buys a stock and writes a CALL against the stock. (See Figure II-4.) Absent some special strategy, the CALL is typically about 10% out-of-the-money. Let's look at an example:

On January 20 I buy 1,000 shares of IBM at $100 a share, investing $100,000. Simultaneously I sell 10 CALLS of the April 110's for two points, taking in $2,000 of premium. Now my net cost per share is only $98. If IBM stock goes over $110 during the following 90 days, absent some action on my part, it will be called away from me (that is, sold to the owner of the CALL) at $110. So there are three possibilities:

(1) IBM stock goes down. In this case I keep the premium, and I am $2,000 better off than had I just bought the stock. Obviously, if I intended to buy IBM stock anyway, selling the CALL was a good move.

(2) IBM stock does not fluctuate very much during the 90 day period. Again, I keep the $2,000 premium, and, coupled with the quarterly dividend of over 4% per annum, I have increased my yield from an approximately 4 % per annum yield to an approximately 12% annualized yield.

(3) IBM stock goes over $110 during the 3 month period. If I allow the stock to be called away (without buying other stock to deliver), I will make a $10,000 capital gain, plus the $2,000 premium, plus any dividend declared during this period. My annualized return will be approximately 50%!

What I gave away was the potential for a really large profit in the IBM stock during the 90 day period. For this reason, the buy-write strategy is not appropriate for those who want to get rich quick.

If the stock goes over $110 and I don't want to sell the stock, I can buy back the CALLS (at a loss) at any time. Of course, the loss is offset by the unrealized gain in the stock price. Or, I can buy back those CALLS and sell other CALLS at a different strike price and in a different time frame. These are strategies which are described in greater detail in the text below.

D. Summary of Simple Strategies

The most simple strategy in options is to buy an option. Most people in the market will tell you that most people who buy an option lose money on it. Certainly in many cases the option buyer hopes to lose money on an option, since the option is purchased as a hedge for some other kind of position, and that position makes a large profit which is only slightly reduced by the cost of the option. I believe that most sophisticated investors, however, will agree that merely buying a PUT or a CALL for the purpose of expecting it to go up in value is rarely a good investment. Naturally, there are special circumstances where the investor has a strong basis for believing that there will be a substantial short term movement in a particular stock or in the market as a whole. In these circumstances the purchase of an option makes sense. In such a situation, the purchase of an option with a risk of loss appropriate for the investor should not be considered as a risky investment, because the risk of loss is limited to the cost of the investment, and therefore can be carefully evaluated by the investor at the initiation of the investment.

The other side of that transaction is to sell an option. Selling an option, by itself, without being hedged or as part of a combination, puts the seller at the risk of a loss which is usually very large compared to the potential profit. Even a non-volatile stock may be subject to a takeover, can have a very substantial increase in a short period of time, and can therefore subject the seller to great risk.

The seller of a naked PUT on any stock, no matter how highly valued for stability, subjects the seller to a substantial risk, since adverse news or information about the company or industry can cause a substantial decline in the value of any stock. Who could have predicted the uncovering of massive fraud either in the Equity Funding Corporation or the Technical Equity Companies, the American Express scandal or the LTV bankruptcy? But to write (sell) a naked stock PUT is a very conservative move as a method of capturing ownership of a stock during a decline, at a price reduced by the premium.

The buy-write is a widely used method of increasing the current income from stock holdings, while giving up only some portion of the upside potential. This technique is a low risk option technique, provided that the investor has already decided to accept the risk of holding the stock. A large capital investment is required to participate in a buy-write and that is its main drawback. For this reason, this strategy is often favored by institutional investors that have the capital available for wide diversification. There are also potential tax drawbacks which are discussed below, under "tax considerations."

The basic option strategies that I consider inappropriate for the conservative investor are the following:

    1. Selling an uncovered stock CALL.

2. Selling more uncovered stock PUTS than you are prepared to convert to long term stock holdings it the stock is put to you.

3. Selling any uncovered index option that is not part of a hedged strategy.

The following basic strategies stand out as those used regularly by professionals to make money in the options market:

1. Acquiring stock at a discount, or during a price dip, by selling PUTS.

2. Selling out-of-the-money CALLS against stocks owned to generate premium income. When the stock is purchased at the same time the CALLS are written, this is called a "buy-write."

E. Basic Principles of Conservative Option Strategies

This book is two books rolled into one: the "how to" explanations, and a philosophical discussion of stock market strategies. As with any philosophy, the one expressed here has a certain number of underlying assumptions. Since we have been engrossed in a lot of "how to" discussion, it is now time to look at the philosophical part, and, particularly, some of these underlying assumptions.

Some of the assumptions are pretty obvious. Investors want to make the best return on their investment commensurate with the degree and dollar amount of risk they are willing to take. In other word, if I can get $3 by investing $1 it is better than if I can get $2 by investing $1, if the risk is the same.

Some of the assumptions in this book are less obvious. I don't think anybody can predict the market with much success. Some people are pretty good at particular stocks, where they either have an inside track on the company, or are willing to devote an extraordinary amount of time and energy in gathering and analyzing information about the company. That's not me. But I do think that one can predict a range of fluctuations in the market with some degree of statistical probability. While there are periods of unusual volatility both in particular stocks and the overall market, this is not true most of the time, and most weeks that go by the market does not move more than one would anticipate from looking at past performance.

I think that it is pretty reasonable to infer some basic principles from these underlying assumptions.

1. First of all, for short term investment it is cheaper and safer to buy CALLS than buy stock. Yet I never do it. Why not? Because I never think of myself as a short term investor in stocks. I always think of myself as a long term investor in stocks.

But, historically I know that is not true. Typically I own stocks for one or two years, and then I am out of that company and into some other one. Typically I am into different industries every two or three years. Right now I am in biotech and certain other high tech stocks. At other times I have been in automotive stocks. Then there was my metals phase.

If I ever came to accept the fact that I really don't hold stocks more than one or two years, and made a cost analysis, I might find out that it would have been cheaper to buy one or two nine month CALLS on the stocks than to buy the stocks themselves. It certainly seems less risky.

When I buy 100 shares of IBM at $120 per share, I put up $12,000. My theoretical potential loss is $12,000. But if I buy in-the-money CALLS, with little time value premium for say, $5,000, I may achieve the same result at a lower theoretical risk and smaller out-of-pocket investment and the same upside potential. Why don't I do it? Because no one buys stock thinking that it is going to go down. So few investors really consider the theoretical risk and cost because they are focused on the profit. In addition, it is hard to find long term in-the-money CALLS that do not have a lot of time value premium in them, and therefore there may not be that many occasions where CALLS can be used in place of stocks.

So that's why I put this discussion in the philosophical,

or "principles" part of this book. This concept may not have a lot of practical value, but it is important to recognize the principle; namely that options control stock in a way that the benefits to be achieved may be just as great or greater with the options, while the cost is much less. One major purpose of this book is to illustrate specific useful examples of this basic principle.

2. The next basic principle in this book is that the most likely way to profit from options is to sell options so as to capture time value premium. Selling options is called "writing." And so option writing is the key to profits as expounded in this book. This basic principle flows naturally from the underlying assumption that no one can accurately predict the market. By analogy, no one can accurately predict when they are going to die. We can judge, based on statistics, the average age we will achieve, depending on various groups in which we fit. As a white male living in Los Angeles smog, I think I have about 20 years to go, statistically. But I would not be willing to invest on that premise.

There are people that do invest according to that premise, however, and they do not really care about me individually, but they know that they can look at a lot of historical data and predict with pretty good accuracy how old several hundred thousand people like me will be at death. These people run insurance companies. And so the insurance company is willing to write a contract (an annuity) which makes money if I live less than 20 years.

They will also write another contract (a life insurance policy) that will make money if I live more than 20 years and lose money if I live less than 20 years. For either of these I pay them a premium.

That is how I view option writing, and that is the basic profit principle in this book. I sell you a contract to buy IBM stock at $120 a share. You pay me a $500 premium in exchange for my contract. I do it every month for 12 months, adjusting the price as IBM stock moves.

Let's say that I know that historically IBM has not moved more than $5 per share in most months. (This is just an example. I have not really looked at the fluctuation of IBM month-by-month, and realize that it may well be more than $5 per share). So, unless there is a fundamental change in the market or in IBM, most months I am going to get to keep the $500. Once in a while I am going to have to pay it back, and perhaps I will have to pay back more. That is exactly what happens to the life insurance company.

3. This leads to the next principle: Because we are operating on a principle which is based on statistical fluctuation, there can be wide variation from the norm. So for 11 months I may keep your $500, and I will be $5,500 ahead. As long as I do not lose more than a reasonable portion of that $5,500 in the twelfth month, my strategy has worked. And, since I never know which month will be the "twelfth month," each month I try to hedge to prevent

me from losing more money than I expect to gain during a year with normal periods of fluctuation.

The implication to draw from this principle is that virtually all option writing should be hedged. In certain strategies the hedge is automatically present in the strategy, such as writing PUTS to acquire stock, and in spreads. But this basic principle must be followed if one is to be philosophically consistent with the premises expressed here.

4. Finally, it seems to follow that writing options on an index is safer than writing on individual stocks, unless the investor has some other reason for owning the stock. For example, some investors are locked into a large stock portfolio which, for tax purposes, they do not want to liquidate. Some investors acquire stock as part of their employment, and are not legally permitted to sell it. And some investors make an investment decision to acquire certain stocks. But if one is investing according to the philosophy expressed above, and writing options to acquire time value premium, writing the options on an index is safer because the diversity of stocks used in the index smoothes out the fluctuation that can arise from significant market information about one company.

Undoubtedly, there are more underlying assumptions and more basic principles in this book than I have spelled out here. Part of the investment process is formulating your own assumptions and reaching your own basic principles from them.

Preface to Parts III and IV
The Transition from the Basics to "Useful" Strategies

The basic option strategies are of importance primarily as a route to understanding options. The only basic strategies that have much practical applications, for purposes of the recommendations in this book, are (1) the use of the naked PUT as an alternative method of acquiring stock below market price, and (2) the buy-write.

The bulk of the really useful strategies are more complex, and rely on combinations of two or more trades at the same time. It is the interplay between the different positions that creates the desired strategic position.

At the beginning of option writing the brain has to consider each of the positions independently, then evaluate what happens when the two results are combined - a three part sequential thinking process. But after a short period of time the option trader sees the combinations as a unit, and knows instinctively what the profit or loss will be at different underlying stock prices.

I do not believe that this level of comprehension can be derived from reading a book. Like swimming or riding a bicycle, it has to be developed experientially. So, after you feel that you understand what you have read, try a few trades - even if they are only on paper and not for real money.

The "complex strategies" fall naturally into two large categories. The first category, to which Part III is devoted, is the writing of CALLS against an underlying position. The most common underlying position is stock, but there are so many different positions to sell calls against, that a whole chapter is required to cover the possibilities. In Part III I have tried to cover the subject in a way that conveys an understanding of the methodology that can be applied to any case. But the simple fact remains that much of Part III is esoterica that most traders will rarely use, important primarily for an understanding of the subject. The basic CALL writing strategy used by most traders is writing CALLS against stock, which is not very different from the buy-write strategy described above.

Let us look at the differences:

In the buy-write, the trader buys stock, and writes an out-of-the-money CALL on the same stock, one option for each 100 shares of stock, at the same time. For example, at the same time I buy 100 shares of IBM at $100 per share, I sell one CALL of IBM with a strike price of 105. (The expiration date is not relevant to the example.)

Generally the stock is purchased as part of a strategy to profit from the premium on the CALL. For example, in the illustration above, the premium might be $100 ($1 times the 100 shares one option represents), and the trader will profit only by the $100 if the price of IBM stock stays the same.

Of course, some traders may do this buy-write in order to acquire the IBM stock at an effective price of $99 per share ($100 cost less the $1 premium) on the theory that the stock will stay the same or go up, but not by $5.

But I believe that most CALL writing is done by institutions for the purpose of improving performance of an underlying portfolio held for long term appreciation. In other words, these institutions are already committed to the idea of buying and holding a diverse portfolio of stocks. Since they hold the stocks anyway, the managers decide to give up the possibility of short term appreciation in excess of say 10%, in favor of increasing income on the portfolio by generating CALL option income. In the example above, the option writer gives up the possibility of benefiting from an increase of IBM stock from $100 per share to more than $105 per share, in exchange for a $100 premium. But he keeps the profit between $100 and $105, as well as the option premium.

So the buy-write strategy is usually used either to acquire stock at a discount, or to capture short-term option premium. The writing of CALLS against an existing stock portfolio is a more common strategy used primarily to increase short-term income on a long-term portfolio.

In Part IV we cover more complex two-or-more-part strategies. Of these, spreads are vastly the most common. And of the spreads, the most common is the "price" spread described in Part IV. The price spread is a relatively simple way to capture premium income with a defined dollar loss risk. The spread is particularly useful as a method of hedged writing, with reasonable margin requirements.

You can understand basic spreads after a few minutes of manipulating numbers with a pen and paper. And an understanding of the basic price spread is essential before the rest of the materials can be readily understood.

So these are the most important strategies to understand for purposes of application:

1. Sale of a PUT to acquire stock.
2. The buy-write.
3. Writing out-of-the-money CALLS against the same underlying stock as the CALL.
4. Writing price spreads to generate premium income from the passage of time.

By acquiring the ability to actually do these four strategies, an understanding of the more complex ones will follow naturally.

PART III - Writing CALLS Against Instruments Other Than Stock

A. Writing CALLS against deep-in-the-money CALLS

Instead of using stock as an instrument to write CALLS against, to limit potential losses, you can buy CALLS - which are much cheaper than buying the stock.

For example:

With Ford at 42, I decide to sell the April 45 CALLS for 1 point. I plan to sell 10 CALLS, for a gross premium of $1,000. I could hedge by buying 1,000 shares of Ford for $42,000.

Alternatively, I can buy 10 CALLS of the Oct. 40's for, say 2 3/4 points, which will cost me $2,750. My increased risk is a drop below 40, at which time I start to incur a potential loss of the whole $2,750 premium I paid for the long position (the 40 CALLS). My hope is to close out both positions in April, keep the $1.00 premium on the 45 CALLS, and sell the long 40 position for approximately what I paid for it.

Obviously, I will be safer if I buy the 35 CALLS instead of the 40's, but then I will put up $5,000 more - still, however much less than buying the stock.

So long as the stock price stays above the long call strike price, a decline in the stock price costs me the same as if I had bought the stock, with one difference: part of whatever time value premium I paid (in my example 3/4 point, or $750) will be lost. That amount may or may not be equal to the use of the money saved by not buying the stock.

B. Private Options and Collars

While the discussions in this book center around publicly traded options, there are a number of private options written each year. Many institutions, primarily banks, provide a service to clients by arranging to buy or sell options from the client on stock which is either not publicly traded, or which is publicly traded but not optionable on any market.

Because of the variety of arrangements that are available, it is beyond the scope of this book to detail them. In addition, the complex strategies employed by the banks and other institutions to hedge such transactions and make them possible is a study in itself. But there is one transaction which is common enough to warrant an explanation here, and it is called the "collar." The collar arises in the public market also, but it is a favorite transaction in private options for the reasons explained below.

Investors are often "stuck" with large stock positions which, for one reason or another, are not practical to sell. Three common examples are (1) where the investor has a very low basis in the stock and doesn't want to pay the capitol gain tax on sale, (2) where the stock is in a family business, and the investor doesn't want to disturb the market by selling a large block, and (3) where the stock is restricted, for example under the Securities and Exchange ("S.E.C.") rules, and cannot be legally sold for some period of time.

By way of illustration, let us consider the third example. Mr. I takes his company public, and retains $10 million worth of stock after the public offering. The stock is restricted and cannot be sold for two years. Mr. I fears that interest rates will move up, and his holdings will decline very substantially before he can legally begin to liquidate the stock.

In this situation, Mr. I may go to a bank that performs private option services, and put a collar on his position. The most common collar would be the purchase of a put, and the simultaneous sale of a call, where the premiums are equal. For example, if Mr. I's stock is trading at $20 per share, the bank might sell him a put with a strike price of $15 per share, and buy a call from him with a strike price of $23 per share, with no cash changing hands. Typically the bank does this either because it can resell its positions and make a small premium on the sale, or because it can buy and sell offsetting options on the market (since it is not subject to the legal restriction) at a slightly less net cost.

Why does Mr. I do this? By buying the puts at a $15 strike price, he is protected against a decline of more than 25% in the stock price. In exchange for this protection, he is giving up any increase in the stock above $23 per share. He is willing to give up this "upside" since he feels that he has a large enough holding, and for the insurance that the holding will not decline below $7.5 million.

The variety of private options which can be tailored for individual needs is amazing, and several banks have experts available to construct such transactions for wealthy stockholders. These institutions also provide such services as purchasing restricted stock (at a discount, usually ranging from 5-15%) under the "offshore" exemption to the S.E.C. rules.

C. Convertible Bonds

Convertible bonds are bonds which have a "kicker" that gives the bond holder the right to exchange the bonds for stock in the company under certain conditions. This "kicker" is very much like an option or a warrant. The nice thing about convertible bonds is that the investment you make pays interest while you are waiting to see if your option becomes valuable. The bad part of convertible bonds is that they usually pay less interest than you could get somewhere else because they have the "kicker" attached to them.

Where the bonds are convertible into optionable stock, some investors mentally cull out the option feature of the bond, treat it like an option, and write other options on the underlying stock in conjunction with the option feature of the convertible bond.

For example, K-Mart 6% July 1999 bonds were convertible to 28.17 shares. That is, each $1,000 face value of bonds could be converted to 28.17 shares of common stock. If the common stock was selling for $30 per share, the conversion value of the bonds would be $845.10. The price of the bond might be $900. This would make the yield 6.6%. In some cases the yield on a convertible bond is greater than that on the stock. The bond can be used to cover the risk of writing options on the stock in place of the stock which has a poorer yield than the bond. Note that the conversion ratio, in this case 28.17, must be considered in determining how many options can be sold. For example, 25 bonds ($25,000 face and $22,500 cost) would be convertible to 25 times 28.17 or 704.25 shares, and could cover writing 7 options on the stock.

It is not part of the philosophy espoused in this book to write options in conjunction with convertible bonds, except insofar as the bonds are treated as a bond portfolio. This is discussed in the section on Hedging Against Interest Rate Fluctuations. Convertible bonds are really a business unto themselves, and to evaluate the underlying option writing potential requires a lot of investigation into the underlying terms of the bond indenture, as well as the company itself. The purchase of the bonds requires a large capital investment, and therefore when writing calls for the purpose of capturing time value premiums, the underlying stock is generally more suitable than the convertible bond.

As shown in the above example, however, if one is inclined to own convertible bonds anyway, one can use them as a vehicle for capturing CALL premiums, while being hedged by the convertible feature of the bonds. The investor should make a careful analysis of the relationship between fluctuation in the stock and the value of the bond to determine the appropriate ratio of CALLS to write against each bond and still remain reasonably hedged.

D. Hedging Against Interest Rate Fluctuations

This strategy is of particular interest to investors with a bond portfolio. The value of bonds fluctuates inversely to interest rates. For example, when a key interest rate is

8%, bond issues which pay 8% will sell at par ($1,000 per bond). If that key rate goes up to 9 %, that bond becomes less valuable. A new investor could buy a bond like the one you bought, for par, and get a 9% return. So he is not going to pay you par for your bond. He will probably only pay you just under $900 for your bond. Then when he gets his $80 return on your bond, he has gotten approximately the same 9% return which he could get somewhere else, since 9% of $900 is $81.

So now that interest rates are at 9%, your bond has dropped from $1,000 value to $900 value. Of course, if interest rates go down to 7%, your bond is more valuable, because now the investor cannot go out and buy a bond that pays 8% for a $1,000 investment.

Whenever the investor with a bond portfolio is primarily interested in conservation of invested capital, with a reasonable rate of return which, at a minimum, will keep up with the rate of inflation, the ideal situation for him is option writing.

To prevent a decrease in the portfolio, one can buy or write options on an interest index so that if interest rates decline, and the bond portfolio goes up in value, the investor has given up that increase by paying out option premiums. Conversely, if interest rates go up, and the value of the bond portfolio declines, the option investor makes a profit on the options which is geared to approximate the loss on the bonds.

Banks often follow this strategy to protect their underlying bond investment portfolio. The bank is not buying the bonds to profit from capital appreciation, but to maintain adequate capital to meet federal regulations. To protect against this capital declining, and thereby falling below the federal regulations, smart banks protect their bank portfolios with options. There are specialists who do nothing but handle this kind of transaction on behalf of banks.

One way to hedge the bond portfolio is to buy options on the interest index. One can also sell interest rate spreads to take in time value premium. Even if you don't have a bond portfolio, you can do that, but if you have a bond portfolio, it is a particularly good way of capturing time value premium and hedge your bond portfolio at the same time. A discussion of the interest index is beyond the scope of this book, since I promised not to make it encyclopedic. Suffice to say that here are two main indexes, one that follows government bond index rates, and one that follows municipal bond index rates. Sometimes it is hard to write options on the municipal bond index, because there is not always much activity, and it sometimes lacks buyers and sellers. The regular interest index has a lot of activity on it, and it is a very highly leveraged market with a lot of speculation. It is very easy to lose a lot of money on it very quickly. It is particularly complicated because the numbers are inverted - that is, when interest rates go up, the index numbers go down and vice versa. It is also complicated because the numbers do not mean what they say, and are not expressed in decimals. So you have to learn a whole new language, and turn your mind upside down.

Writing options on an interest index is not for the faint of heart, but for those who want to study it a little more I present the following actual example of a typical interest rate spread:

On May 4, 1991 Treasury Bond Futures were quoted:

May 90 0-53 May 92 0-13

This means that a May 90 Treasury Bond Future was priced at 53/64 or $828.10 per contract. The May 92's were 13/64 or $203.10 per contract.

The following spread was put on:

Sold 10 May 90's $8,281 credit

Bought 10 May 92's   (2,031) cost

Gross credit $6,250

less $350 per position commission

    (700)

NET PROCEEDS $5,550

The hope was that interest rates would go up and the value of the contracts would decrease. If interest rates increased so that the price was below $90 per hundred (in $100,000 increments) the futures would expire worthless and the net proceeds could be kept.

However, interest rates declined and the price of the contracts increased. The price of the May 90's at the close of the contracts was 1-36 or 1 and 36/64ths. The May 92's expired worthless.

The cost of buying back the 10 May 90 Treasury Bond contracts was $15,625 plus $350 commission or $15,975.00.

The final result of this spread was a loss of $15,975 less the initial net proceeds of $5,550 - a $10,220 loss. As I said, writing options on an interest index is not for the faint of heart.

E. Long Term Options

Long term options are relatively new, and few of us have had long experience with them at this point. The principles of selling long term options should be exactly the same as selling traditional options, and the question to be investigated is whether the ratio of time value premium to historical stock volatility is at least as much as with traditional options. The amount of time value premium for the remaining life of the option is a key factor in the potential profitability of a writing strategy. This figure is often influenced by demand.   As long term options become more popular, I would expect to see the time value premium on options on volatile stocks expand.

The following is an example of a trade which was made with long term options:

On May 16, 1991 the following long term CALL options on IBM were available:

1/93 105	13 5/8
1/93 135	5 3/8
1/93 165	2 1/8
7/92 135	4
7/92 85	23

IBM was trading at $102 1/2.

June IBM 105 CALLS were trading at 2 1/2. If IBM were to remain below $105 these would expire worthless. It would be possible to buy a January 1993 IBM 105 for 13 5/8 and use this to cover writing of the June 105's. After these expired the August 105's could be written, etc. The cost of the long term option to cover these writes would be only 13 5/8 rather than $102.50 for the stock. Of course, the option would not pay a dividend. However, if

IBM fell to $80 per share the loss on shares purchased at $102.50 would be $22.50 per share, while the loss on the January 1993 option would only be the $13.62 per share that the option cost.

PART IV - Combination and Complex Strategies for Conservative Investors

First let me assure you that I am not going to discuss in this text all of the really fancy strategies used in the options market. Those of you active in the market have certainly heard of strips and straps, strangles and reverse repo hedging. I am not doing that here. I am only going to discuss a few of the most commonly used option strategies. There are enough of those to keep us very busy and there are not that many people who understand even those few that we discuss here. The common threads of these strategies are: (1) each has a defined risk; and, (2) in each, we expect to profit by capturing time value premium from the sale of an option.

A. Spreads

Spreads are pretty complicated because there are so many different kinds. Again, the vocabulary of spreads is what makes it difficult for most people to think about them.

FIGURE IV-1 Calendar and Price Spread
(Out-of-the money)

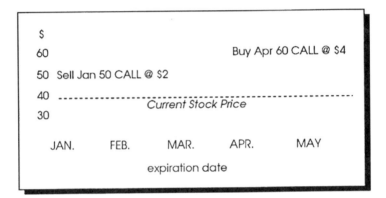

If you collect a $2 premium on the sale and pay out a $4 premium on the purchase, this is a "debit spread," where you have a $2 debit at the opening. If the stock price stays below $50 when the January option expires you will be able to close out the April option and keep the premium collected on the January option. The risk of loss is small, because (1) there is a large "window" (10 points), and (2) if the stock price goes beyond $50, the April position value will increase so the sale of it will cover some of the loss of the January position.

Premiums this high would only be available in a stock viewed by the Market as quite volatile.

I am not sure that it is necessary to know the vocabulary of spreads to make money from doing them. But if you make money from doing them and want to talk about them to your friends, here goes.

A basic concept of the spread is that there are two options which have some relationship. The relationship usually is that both positions are on the same stock, and are designed to act together in some way that accomplishes a goal. For the moment, let's take the simple cases and define spreads as two options on the same security. With this starting point, spreads can be classified in a number of ways.

Calendar Spreads. The calendar spread is a combination of two options with the same strike price and a different expiration date. In other words, the two parts of the spread consist of options that expire on different calendar dates. An example of the calendar spread is the sale of a Ford 50 CALL expiring in January and the purchase of a Ford 50 CALL expiring in April. (See Figure IV-1.)

One main reason for entering into a calendar spread is to take advantage of the time value decline line. Since an option loses all of its time value premium by expiration date, there is some amount of time value premium that it loses on each trading day between the day the buyer sells it and the date it expires. In other words, if you buy for $2 an out-of-the-money option ten trading days before it expires and it stays out-of-the-money, it will lose $2 of value in the ten remaining trading days. But it will probably not lose 20 cents on each of those ten days. Time value changes depending partly on the price of the stock, that is, how far out-of-the-money it stays, and there is also a tendency for the value to depreciate more quickly the closer it is to the expiration date. Generally speaking, most of the time value premium seems to disappear during the last 30 days of an option's life, and the decline in value seems to accelerate quickly during the last two or three weeks of its life. See Figure I-6.

For this reason, some investors seeking to capture time value premium write calendar spreads by selling a short term position such that the premium expires quickly, and buying a longer term position to hedge, which does not lose much time value premium if closed out when the earlier position expires.

Price Spread. A price spread is where the expiration date of both positions is the same, but the strike price is different. For example: When Ford is at $45, I sell a Ford 50 CALL and buy a Ford 55 CALL, both expiring in 30 days. The purpose of such a spread is to capture the time-value premium of the 50 CALL, while limiting the risk to five points (between $50 and $55). We will examine such reasoning when we talk about the purposes for spreads below. Fig. IV-1 shows a combination calendar and price spread.

Bull and Bear Spreads. Another way to characterize spreads is as "bull spreads" and "bear spreads." The "bull spread" is a spread in which the investor makes a profit if the underlying stock or index goes up; the "bear spread" is a spread in which the investor will lose money if the underlying stock or index goes up and make money if the underlying stock or index goes down. It is convenient to think about spreads in terms of bull or bear, just to check your hypothesis in investing.

Here is an example of a common bull spread (see Figure IV-2):

With Hitachi at $99, I sell 10 of the 100 PUTS and buy 10 of the 90 PUTS to hedge, for a net credit of $6,000. If Hitachi goes up over 100 (and stays there) until expiration, I make $6,000. My risk of loss is $10,000 less $6,000, or $4,000.

Here is an example of a bear spread (see Figure IV-3):

With Monsanto at $101, I sell one 100 CALL and buy one 105 CALL, for a net credit of $200. This is a bear spread because it profits if the stock goes down, but loses if the stock goes up. The worst case is a rise over $105, which will result in a net loss of $300, $500 less the $200 premium.

Most CALL spreads are bear spreads.

Credit and Debit Spreads

A credit spread is one where the option sold creates

FIGURE IV-2 Bull Spread.

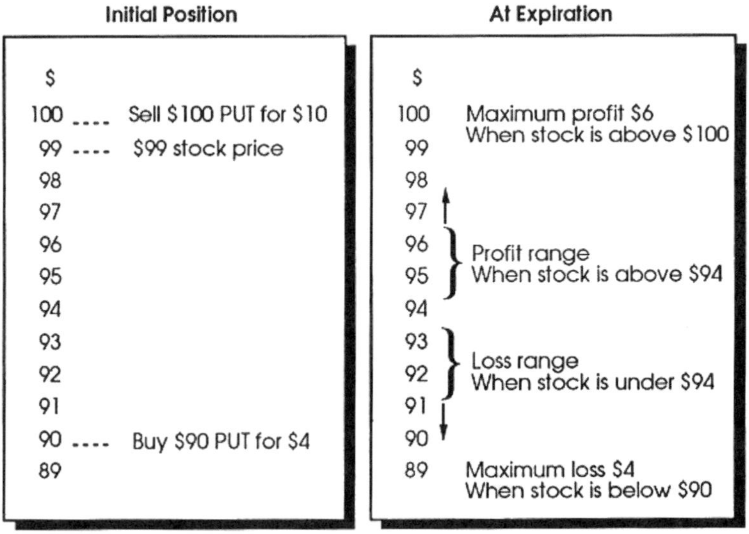

This is a _Bull Spread_ because (1) you are short and long the same security at a different price, creating a spread, and (2) it's "bullish" because you profit when the security goes _up_ and lose when it goes _down_.

more premium than the option bought when the position is put on. (See Figure IV-4). For example, most price spreads are credit spreads, because you sell the option at the closer strike price - therefore more valuable - and buy the cheaper option at the further strike price.

A debit spread is where you pay out money when the spread is placed. A calendar spread is typically a debit spread where you buy the option with more time left on it that the one you sell. To profit from this kind of spread your prediction of the stock price has to be accurate. For that reason I don't recommend them. I recommend spreads that capture time value premium when the under-lying stock or index does not fluctuate more than within a certain range.

Like price spreads and calendar spreads, these terms are only helpful for purposes of discussing spreads; none of these terms helps in understanding the reason behind the decision to make investment in the spread. For that reason, I prefer to classify spreads in two categories: (1) spreads to reduce the cost of a primary position, and (2) spreads to hedge a position. Let's take a look at an example of each.

Spreads to reduce the cost of a primary position

Let's assume that Ford stock is at $45. I plan to buy ten CALLS of the Ford 50's expiring in approximately 90 days. I do this because I think that Ford will go up 10 to

FIGURE IV-3 Bear Spread.

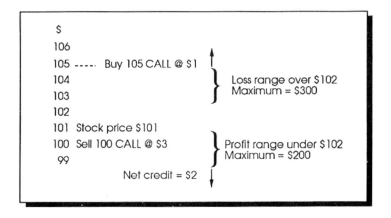

In this example, the 100 CALL is sold and the 105 CALL bought for a net credit of $2 per option. The maximum loss per option is $300 if the stock goes above $105 ($500 minus the $200 premium received). If the stock declines in value below $100 the profit is $200 for each option contract. Some additional profit might be made by selling the long 105 position before expiration.

This is a "bear" spread because you make money if the stock goes down.

20% in the next 90 days, that is, up to the range of $50 to $54. The CALLS cost $2, so for ten CALLS (controlling 1,000 shares) I pay $2,000. I expect to make as much as $2,000 (doubling my money) if my presumption is right and Ford goes up to $54. In other words, if Ford goes up to $54, the 50 CALLS I bought will be $4 in-the-money and worth $4,000 at expiration, so I take in $4,000 and will have paid out $2,000. In order to reduce my cost, however, and increase my potential percentage return, at the same time, I sell 10 Ford 55 CALLS. For this sale I receive 50 cents, or $500 for ten CALLS. Now I am long the Ford 50's, and short the Ford 55's, a sort of bull price spread. My cost is now only $1,500, or 25% less than if I only bought the Ford 50's. I have a risk of loss of 1.5 points, or $1,500. My maximum gain is limited to $3,500 ($5,000 less the $1,500 cost) by the 55 CALLS sold because if Ford goes over $55 the 55 CALL will lose the same amount as any further profit from the 50 CALLS. (See Figure IV-5.)

Spreads to hedge a position

Suppose that telephone stock is at $45. I sell the 50 CALLS 30 days out. I do this because I do not expect telephone to go up 5 points during the next 30 days. Nevertheless, I am uncomfortable about it. If telephone becomes a takeover candidate, the stock might go to $70 or $80. To protect, or hedge my position, I buy the 55 CALLS with the same expiration date. Assuming I have bought and sold ten of each, my maximum loss is now

FIGURE IV-4 An Out-of-the-Money
PUT (Credit) Spread.

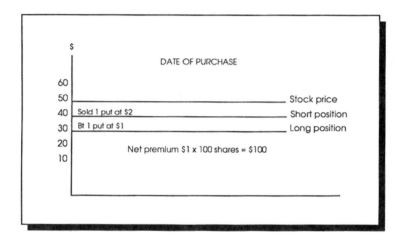

If stock stays above 40 until expiration, seller keeps a $100 premium ($100 per put because 1 put equates to 100 shares).

If stock goes below 40, the buyer of the 40 PUT will "put" the stock to seller, forcing seller to buy 100 shares at $40, no matter how low the stock falls. The seller can either take delivery of the stock, buy back the option before expiration, or buy the stock on the market to deliver to the buyer. (Note that the "seller" of the option becomes the equivalent of a "buyer" of the stock, if "put").

Between 30–40, seller is at risk up to $900 (10 points times 100 shares less $100 premium received).

Below 30 the seller profits $100 on the 30 PUT for each additional $100 of loss on the 40 PUT.

$5,000 less the net premium received on the spread. Until expiration day, if telephone stays between $45 and $50, I get to keep all of the net premium. Between $50 and $55 I will lose $1,000 per point, less the net premium I received. Over $55 my long 55 CALL will gain intrinsic value the same amount that my short 50 CALL loses for each point that the stock goes up. I have limited my risk to a fixed dollar maximum. This is one of the key factors in conservative option investing.

B. Pricing Issues In Writing Spreads

One of the most important decisions to be made by the investor who is writing options spreads for premium income is "is it worth it?" In other words, is the amount of premium worth the risk of loss? Some sophisticated investors use a computer model for this analysis. Such a model uses investor-entered parameters to evaluate the risk and likely extent of loss, and compares the ratio of maximum loss to premium received.

Most of us have to just use a rule of thumb. In writing spreads on an index, my rule of thumb is that I expect that my maximum likely loss will not be more than twice the premium I take in. Then I try to write the spread sufficiently far out of the money such that I believe there is not more than a two-to-one likelihood of the worst case occurring.

For example, some time ago the Hong Kong index was

**FIGURE IV-5 Spread to Reduce the Cost of a
Primary Position (Unusual)**

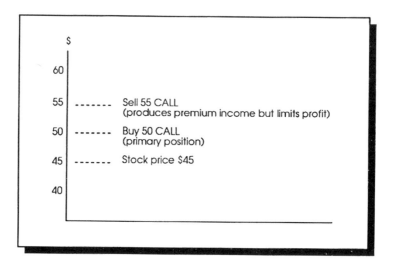

attracting attention. It stood at approximately 258. The investor can sell 10 (out of the money) calls, December 270, and buy 10 calls, December 280, for a credit of $4,250—call it $4,000 after commissions. The underlying assumption is that the market will not go up more than 16 points by the December expiration date (12 points to 270 plus the 4 points of premium received).

At first blush this would not seem to meet the suggested rule of thumb, since there is a 10 point spread, and thus a potential loss of $10,000, and a $4,000 net premium, the ratio is 40%, not 50%.

But the spread writer must look at the potential loss somewhat differently: if the index goes up, the short position (here, the 270) will increase in value, creating a prospective loss. At the same time, the long position (here, the 280) will increase in value, creating a prospective profit. This will be true for most of the life of the spread, except for the last 2-3 weeks when the time value will wane.

This means that for most of the life of the spread, if the worst case comes true and the index goes to 280 or higher, creating the maximum possible loss on the short position, there will nevertheless be some gain on the long position. From experience one can estimate that to be, perhaps, one point (a lot depends on when this sharp rise occurs in the life cycle of the spread). So, the real maximum LIKELY loss is more like $9,000 or so, not $10,000,

FIGURE IV-6 The Box Spread.

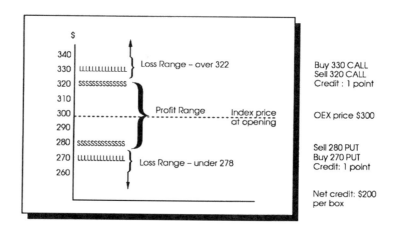

At expiration (except in cases of premature assignment):

> Between 280 and 320 seller keeps the premium.
> Over 322 and under 278 seller loses $100 per point.

The maximum profit is $200 and the maximum loss is $800 ($1,000–$200) on the entire position.

While twice as much premium is collected compared to a single spread, the risk of any loss occurring has also doubled. The potential amount of loss is slightly mitigated because at expiration there can only be a loss on one of the spreads.

In this illustration, the line of "L's" stands for "Long", and line of "S's" stands for "short".

and the ratio of premium to likely loss is better than 50%—a good trade (if you are bearish on the Hong Kong market).

C. Boxes

Now that you are familiar with spreads, it is time to extend that concept to the "box." A box is a combination of two spreads, one on each side of the current price of the underlying stock or index. (See Figure IV-6.)

Let us look at an example:

With the OEX at $300, I put on a CALL spread by selling a 320 CALL (short) and buying a 330 CALL (long). Then I put on a PUT spread where I sell a 280 PUT and buy a 270 PUT. On the CALL spread I might have received $2.00 on the 320 and paid $1.00 for buying the 270, for a net credit of $1.00. Likewise, on the put spread, I may have received $2.00 credit for selling the 280, and paid $1.00 for buying the 270, for a net credit of $1.00. On a typical transaction of ten of each position, I should therefore get a net credit of at least $2,000. Let us look at the effect of putting on this box:

Assume that these are all 30 day positions. If the OEX stays between the range of $280 and $320 during the next 30 days, I keep the $2,000 in net premium. All of the positions, including the long positions, will expire worthless. In other word, I will have made a profit of $4,000 on the short positions, and lost $2,000 on the long positions.

The box exposes you to greater risk than the simple spread (contrary to what many brokers will tell you). With the box, you have twice the chance to lose in case of unexpected volatility. But because the stock (or index) can only end up either up or down - not both - the box is safer than writing two unrelated spreads and is therefore appropriate, in my opinion, for the investor who writes spreads repeatedly.

D. The In-And-Out Strategy

As a result of writing uncovered PUTS on selected stocks, investors are sometimes "put" the stock and thereby become the proud owners of that stock. This has led to a strategy I call "in-and-out," in which the investor keeps writing PUTS until put the stock, then writes CALLS until the stock is called away. The process is repeated until the stock is at a price (either through price change or change of the investor's perception of the company) at which there is insufficient premium in the PUT, at a desirable strike price, to make the strategy profitable.

Here is an example:

Having investigated MCA stock, I become convinced that it has an intrinsic value of $60 which will someday be realized. The stock now sells for $53. At $50 I decide it is a bargain. On February 10 I sell 10 PUTS of the March

50's, for 2 points, receiving $2,000 in premium.

MCA now drops to $48 and in March I am put 1,000 shares.

I now sell the April 50 CALLS and collect $1500 in premium. At this point I own 1,000 shares for which I paid $50,000 and have collected $3,500 in premium, so my net cost is approximately $47 after transaction costs.

If the stock goes to $50 and is called away from me, I let it go, and may start the process over with a new PUT position.

If the stock continues to decline, I continue to write CALLS against it. If I believe the decline is serious, I may write the 45 CALL, collecting some intrinsic value as a hedge against the continued decline in the stock price, particularly if there is no significant premium in the 50 CALL, as the stock moves down.

If the stock goes below $45. I write the 45 CALLS planning to roll up to the 50's when the stock rebounds.

If the stock stays below $45 and I become convinced that it will not recover in the near future, I may hold the stock or I may sell it, to free up capital and take a $5,000+ loss in the stock, which will be partially or fully made up in the premium income. Note: With volatile stocks the drop can be substantially more than the premium income. Nevertheless, I consider this a reasonably conservative strategy, because it seems to me to be significantly safer in terms of capital protection than buying stock at the market and holding it for long-term appreciation.

E. Option Strategies For Mitigating Losses

(1) Strategies after selling a put and the stock declines.

Suppose the investor, perhaps following one of the strategies suggested in this book, sells a put on HWP at a strike price of 50, collecting 3 points of premium. The implied assumption is that the investor is happy to own the stock at 47.

Now suppose that the stock declines to 45. One mitigating strategy at that point in time is to **sell a call in or at the money.**

For example, the investor may sell a call at a strike price of 45, collecting another 3 points. Now the investor has collected 6 points of premium, and is in the same position or better as originally desired, so long as the stock is at 44 or above.

If the stock drops below 44, the strategy can be repeated by buying back the 45 calls (at a profit, since the calls decline in value as the stock declines) and selling the next lower strike price, to pick up a new premium.

If the stock starts back up, the investor is hedged between 45 and 50 in our original example. That is because for each point that the stock goes up, between 45 and 50, the investor earns $1 per share on the in-the-money put, and loses $1 per share on the out-of-the-money call.

If the stock goes over 50, the investor will continue to lose $1 per share on the call, but will not earn $1 per share on the call. For that reason, the call should be bought back at 50. *Cessante ratione, cessit ipsa lex.* (Loosely, "when there's no more reason for what you are doing, knock it off."

The need for this strategy occasionally arises in a different context. When HNZ was approximately 42, the company announced a meeting to discuss future company strategy. In anticipation of the meeting the stock went up to approximately 45. Some investors wanted to take advantage of what they considered an unusual peak in the stock, without giving up the the their long term position.

Some of these investors sold the stock at 45, and simultaneously sold the 45 puts (controlling the same amount of stock as they previously held), taking in a premium of 2 1/2 points. They had taken a profit on their stock (at favorable tax rates) and liberated a substantial amount of capital, while remaining in the same equity position, but with a new effective cost of $42.50 per share.

The implied assumption by the investor when selling the put was that the stock would not dip below $42.50 per share. In fact, after the meeting, the stock dropped to approximately $40 per share. To mitigate this loss of value in the put position, and to protect the premium collected, the investor could sell the 40 calls, and collect in an additional 2 points of premium. By so doing, the investor is returned to approximately the position he or she had anticipated when doing the original trade.

Note that in these examples I did not set forth the time period, or expiration date of the options. That is because it is not relevant to the examples. What is relevant, however, is the fact that generally the calls written to mitigate against a decline should not be longer in time than the put which is outstanding. If the put is a long-term put, the calls might be for a shorter term than the put. Whether or not that is possible depends on how much premium one can receive for the calls, and if it is enough to make the trade worthwhile, and enough to meet the investor's needs for the transaction. Generally speaking, the shorter the time period of the call the better, if the premium is sufficient to do the job. If the call expires and the put is still alive, another call can be written if a mitigating strategy is still called for.

F. Straddles and Rolling-Rewrite Strategies

Straddles are another way to benefit from volatility or lack of volatility, depending on whether you buy or sell them. To buy a traditional straddle the investor buys an option with a strike price on each side of the market,

FIGURE IV-7 Straddle.

BUYER'S VIEWPOINT

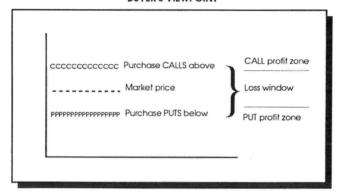

The buyer expects the market to be volatile, and pass beyond the option strike prices during the life of the options.

The profit window for the seller is wider than for the buyer because the buyer pays the Time Value Premium and the seller receives it. The seller is at high risk.

SELLER'S VIEWPOINT

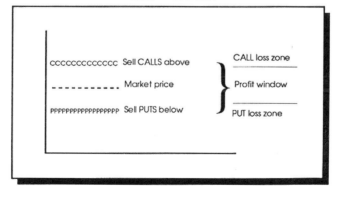

thereby benefiting from a change in price over a certain percentage during the life of the option. (See Figure IV-7.)

For example:

With the OEX at $300, I buy 10 CALLS of the 310's and I buy 10 PUTS of the 290's. I pay $4,000 in premium. I profit if the market goes over $314 or under $286. Just before the war in Iraq, some brokers were recommending the purchase of an OEX 290 PUT, coupled with the sale of the 280 PUT to reduce the cost, on the theory that war would cause the market to plummet. As we know, at the outset of the war the market jumped over 130 points on the Dow Jones Industrial Average in two days. Even without hindsight the straddle was a better selection of investment.

If both options are reversed (the PUT above the market and the CALL below), the options are in-the-money and the risk is point-for-point with the market. This is sometimes called a strangle.

A somewhat popular strategy is to write a straddle (really a straddle/strangle) on the OEX at the money, hedging the downside risk (but usually not the upside) against catastrophe and rewriting on a rolling-rewrite basis (once a week, or once a month). At least one major NYSE brokerage firm currently supports several of its brokers in providing this service to investors with at least $1 million

FIGURE IV-8 The "Unhedged" Combination:
A Misunderstood, High Risk Strategy.

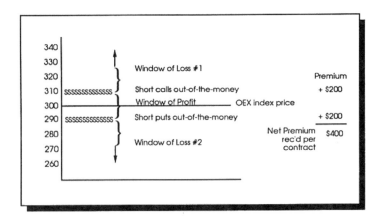

Some investors — and brokers! — are confused by this strategy. They think that because a short position is written on both sides, they are hedged. In fact, by writing on both sides the risk of loss has been doubled, and the only hedge is the extra $200 of premium. That's not much hedge for a potential loss of several thousand dollars!

Note the two large windows of loss.

to invest in the market. It is contended that statistically the market will not deviate as much as the premiums will support if this strategy is followed. Historically this may well be true, but there are two risks to this kind of investment which you should always factor in:

RISK #1. To maintain the kind of discipline required for any rolling strategy requires a substantially full-time market watch. It is not for the person who takes an occasional vacation. Therefore, this kind of strategy is best left to professionals to handle.

RISK #2. Some would-be gamblers try to beat Las Vegas by doubling-up their bet each time they lose. This usually works for awhile, but eventually a streak of bad luck will cause the bet to be too high - either for the bettor or for the house limit and at that point the bettor is broke.

This can also happen in these rolling strategies. At some point a major or sustained rise or drop will occur and even with discipline in closing out losses, your capital can be depleted to the point where you can no longer continue the strategy.

For these reasons I am wary of these rolling strategies, even when professionally handled, and would only invest in them if my capital were pooled with others, the load from such a pool were not excessive and the pool kept ample reserves to continue investing in the face of a significant loss.

FIGURE IV-9 The "PUT and CALL Spread" Combination

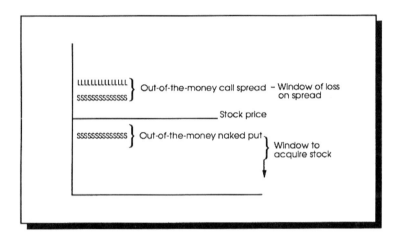

This combination is for the bearish investor who is willing to acquire the stock if it drops, at a price reduced by both a PUT premium and a premium from a CALL spread. The investor is multi-hedged: Hedged against loss on the CALL spread with the PUT premium, and hedged against being put the stock by both premiums.

G. Open Combinations [NOT Really Conservative]

Many option writers (but vastly fewer now than before the October 1987 crash!) sell an out-of-the-money CALL and an out-of-the-money PUT on stocks and the OEX. (See Figure IV-8.) Properly structured such a strategy makes sense, although it is not a conservative investment.

For example: suppose I consider Hitachi, currently at $105, a bargain at $100, and I would be willing to own 100 shares at that price. In lieu of just selling a 100 PUT, I also sell a 110 CALL. I take in $2 on each side, for $4 net. If Hitachi goes to $100 or below, I own it at a net cost of $96 per share. If it appears to be going over $114 I take a small loss (at, say, $112) and roll up the combination to a 105 PUT and a 120 CALL. If I can carefully watch the stock, and it does not run up too fast, this can be a successful strategy on specially selected stocks with adequate premiums. (See Figure IV-9.) But the conservative investor hedges the short CALL with a long CALL - in this case, by buying the 120 or 125 at the outset. (See Figure IV-10.)

The same strategy can be followed on the OEX, but here the conservative investor always hedges the downside with a long position and keeps well out-of-the-money on the CALL side.

Hedging on the upside is thought by some to be less necessary because of two factors:

(1) the potential to partially hedge against a steep increase by maintaining a broad portfolio; and

(2) historically, major declines have been more precipitous and created more disruption in pricing than major increases.

These kinds of open combination can be appropriate for very aggressive option investors who carefully control the amount of risk and are consistently in touch with the market.

H. Three Way "Buy-Write" Combinations

Some very conservative investors add protection to the buy-write strategy. In the buy-write, the investor buys stock and writes out-of-the-money CALLS against it (as described in Part 2-C). The major risk of loss is that the stock price will fall more than the CALL premium. To protect against that, in some cases it makes sense to buy an out-of-the-money PUT, to hedge against a decline in the stock price (See Figure IV-10). This usually only makes good sense when the net CALL premium is greater than the net PUT premium.

Mervyn L. Hecht

FIGURE IV-10   The "Three-way" Combination.

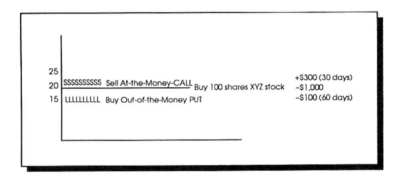

This investor is trying to capture a high-risk (and therefore high premium) CALL premium, hedged on the upside with the stock and on the downside with the long PUT.

If the stock goes up in the next 30 days, it will be called away at cost, and the investor will sell the PUT and keep the net premium on the CALL, less the loss on the PUT (decline in value over 30 days of its 60 day life).

If the stock goes down, the PUT value will increase, offsetting some of that loss.

The main problem with this strategy is that commissions usually eat up the potential profits.

PART V - Mitigating Strategies and Taking Profits and Losses

As soon as you put on your positions, a moment later they may change dramatically. When this happens, you are faced with various decisions, which are typically as follows:

1. Do nothing;
2. Take a profit and terminate further risk;
3. Accept a loss or allow a losing position to continue to escalate;
4. Hedge a winning or losing position;
5. Start over with a new position;
6. Increase or decrease a position.

I believe that it is in this decision making process that most option writers lose money. They typically lose by deviating from their basic premise (capturing premium) and because of an unwillingness to accept loss.

A. Understanding The Psychology Of Loss

There is some compulsion that drives people in our society to try and recoup losses through the same process in which the losses were generated - even if it is illogical to think that such a process is likely to result in recouping the losses. Thus, the gambler who loses in roulette typically tries to recoup his losses in roulette and not by switching to the crap table. Indeed, if the gambler does change games, he or she often considers the loss to be taken and the change is viewed as a new start.

This psychological compulsion has had some very sad effects on investors in the stock market. Some investors - including professional money managers and sophisticated investors - having developed a particular strategy, will continue to employ a losing strategy rather than change to a new strategy.

The investor in options must be careful not to fall into this, or any other, form of compulsive behavior. In market terminology this is called "discipline." The option trader should try and exercise discipline and see things for what they are.

There is a second psychological component which seems to play a part in the psychology of option writing. As a child I used to bet with my friends on the flip of a coin. If after flipping the coin five times the coin came up heads each of those five times, I was more likely to bet on

tails on the sixth flip of the coin. All competent statisti-
cians will tell you that the sixth flip of the coin is not different statistically than each of the prior five flips. That is,
there is a 50-50 chance that the coin will come up heads
on the sixth flip just as there was on each of the prior flips.
Yet, the human mind somehow ascribes a higher likelihood to change than not change.

This false perception also plays a part in the market.
Many option writers are trapped into believing that when
the market goes up, it must come back down. Many of
these beliefs are codified into popular market slogans,
such as "what goes up must come down."

Because of the limited life of options, even if the saying
is true (and it isn't), it doesn't apply to option writing. As
the market goes up, it can continue to go up well beyond
the expiration date of the options. It can go up beyond the
expiration date of the new options written as the old
options begin to lose money. It can go up and up and up,
while some make money and some lose money, just as it
can go down and down and down.

Therefore, in determining when to modify an option
position before expiration, the important consideration
should be to maintain the same strategy as originally con-
ceived and to limit and reduce the risk of loss. The general principles to follow in this connection are:

1. When an option position begins to lose money, close it out.

2. In rolling an option position (the meaning of this is discussed below) ask yourself the question: "Is this an appropriate initial position to put on, irrespective of what has happened in the past?"

3. Also ask yourself the question: "Is this new position consistent with my original strategy?"

The most important single aspect of the psychology of option writing is to recognize that option writing is a statistical process. The option writer tries to capture premiums based on accepting risk. Accepting risk means that there will be some losses and some profits. The option writer must therefore be willing to accept losses and base the expectation of profit on there being more profit positions written than loss positions.

B. Margin and Commission Considerations

After self-reflection, the next most important consideration in modifying an option position may be commissions. Commissions are the nasty topic rarely dealt with in option treatises. The custom seems to be to acknowledge that illustrations exclude transactions costs, including commissions, and to briefly mention the fact that commissions can be a significant factor in option writing.

In fact, commissions can very often be the determining factor in option writing as to whether or not the writer makes a profit or a loss. In writing options between 10 and 50 contracts, the most favorable commission structure that I have ever been able to negotiate is to pay approximately $25 commission for each 10 contracts traded. This is only $0.025 per share. A typical charge for a top non-institutional investor in today's competitive market is $0.04 per share. This comes to $100 per 25 contracts, or $800 in putting on and closing out a 25 contract box spread. I know that some institutional investors pay less than that, and I know that some institutional investors have particular arrangements with brokerage houses where they only pay a commission on opening the option transaction, and nothing on closing it. It is not uncommon, however, for investors to pay as much as a $120 commission for each 10 contracts.

An option writer writing a box spread, which consists of four separate options at a time, can therefore be paying almost as much in commissions (if the box spread is opened and all of the position subsequently closed out) as is collected in premiums! This would make it very difficult to earn a profit from writing. For this reason, it is almost mandatory that the serious option writer negotiates a reduced commission structure with the broker.

Commissions become an important factor in option writing in the determination of closing out a profit position. For example, suppose that when the OEX was $320, I wrote 10 CALL spreads, selling the 330's and buying the 340's. Now the market drops precipitously to $280. Both my long and short positions have declined in value, the short position now costing 1/8th of a point and the long position having a value of 1/16th of a point: so the spread could be closed out for a cost of 3/16, or $37.50 plus commissions. With commissions, the net cost of closing out this position will be say, $117.50.

If I do nothing, the options will expire worthless unless the market rebounds past $330. If I close out the position, I will lock in a profit of my net premium less $117.50.

Which decision I make obviously will depend on my judgment at the time, which will, of course, include such factors as the length of time remaining on the options and the commission cost to close out the position. One choice which is commonly made in this situation is to close out the short position, which is the only position at risk, at a cost of $66.25, and leave the long position in place, in the vague hope that the market could strongly rebound and the position either generate a profit or be utilized again as a hedge for writing a new short position of significant premium.

Another decision to make is whether or not to use a discount broker or a full service broker. If you can watch the market each day while your positions are on, obviously the least expensive broker is an advantage. But if you are not on top of the market you may need a full service broker. The full service broker will call you if a problem is imminent, and will work on getting trades made within a range of discretion, which most discount brokers will not do. And if I'm out of touch for a few days, I feel safer leaving instructions with a broker I know well and speak with frequently. Never-the-less, I know option traders who use discount brokers without problems and save a great deal of money on commissions.

Along with commissions, each brokerage house sets margin requirements, some of which are mandated by federal law and some by stock exchange rules. In considering option writing you should be sure to have adequate capital to cover the "worst case." Many option writers maintain a stock or bond portfolio in the option account to cover margin requirements. Options are then written to hedge against a decline in the bond values (because of an increase in interest rates) and CALLS are written against the stocks. The underlying portfolio thus does double-duty.

C. Recognizing Loss - Accepting A "Fresh Start"

The most important damage control mechanism in writing options is to close out a position at a predetermined loss. Thus, many out-of-the-money option writers decide in advance (and may even instruct the broker in advance) to close out a spread when the short position is at-the-money. For example:

FIGURE V-1 Rolling Up a CALL Spread That Gets In-the-Money.

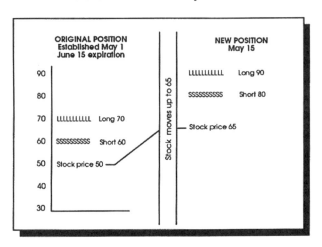

Typical prices – prices at 10 options:

Original position:	Received for $60 short CALLS	$1,000
	Paid for $70 long CALLS	$500
	NET RECEIVED	$500

To close out original position:

	Paid to buy back $60 short CALLS	$7,000
	Received from sale of $70 CALLS	$4,000
	Loss	($3,000)
	Net loss so far	($2,500)

Received on new spread $500

If the new spread is "rolled out" to a calendar date beyond June 15th, $1,000 or more might be received, further mitigating the losses.

When the OEX is at $300, I sell the 310 CALLS and buy the 320's. When the OEX moves up to $310, I close out the position at a loss, by buying back the 310 CALLS (at a cost greater than I sold them) and selling the 320's (at a slight profit, perhaps). By closing out the position before the short position becomes in-the-money, I pay out only the increased difference in the time value premium and avoid paying out any intrinsic value premium.   Each investor should make a decision as to how much loss should be accepted when putting on a position. This decision should be determined by such factors as the amount of premium received on the position and the potential risk of allowing the position to get in-the-money. For example, if a $3,000 premium was received for a spread with a maximum potential loss of $5,000, the investor would be more likely to allow the position to get in-the-money than in the case where a relatively small premium, compared to potential loss, has been received.

D. Rolling A Position Up or Down

When the position has been closed out, a common loss mitigation strategy is to roll the position up or down. (See Figure V-1.) At the same time, the position can be rolled "out," which means to a later calendar date, thereby capturing a new, larger premium.

When I close out the position described above (short OEX 310 and long OEX 320), I now write a new CALL spread which is again approximately 10 points out-of-the-money: I sell the 320 CALLS and buy the 325's or 330's. If the new CALL spread has the same expiration date as the old CALL spread, I have rolled up the CALL spread. If I write the new position for a later calendar date, I have rolled "up and out."

Obviously the same strategy can be employed with PUTS: On May 1 I write a June Put spread when the OEX is at $300; I sell the 290 PUTS and buy the 280 PUTS. By May 15 the OEX has declined to $289. I now close out the original PUT spread and write a new PUT spread by selling the 280's and buying the 270's. I made a profit on the long 280 PUTS, but lost considerably more on the 290 short positions. But the loss was made up by the premium from the new spread. Unless the market declines below $280 I will not lose any money, but I also will not garner the premium I had hoped to keep from the sale of the first spread.

In volatile markets, where the need to roll a position is likely, some option writers take more risk at the outset by writing a wider spread, in the anticipation of having to roll it up or down. By leaving more room in the spread, the same long position can be maintained, a greater initial premium received because of the reduced cost of the long position and commissions can be reduced by not having to close out the initial long position.

For example: When the OEX is at $300, I sell the 310 CALLS and buy the 330 CALLS. I get a good premium on the 310's, because it is close to the money and pay very little for the 330's, which are way out-of-the-money. If the market moves up, I can buy back the 310's and write the 315's, 320's, or the 325's. I have room to roll up three different times if it becomes necessary. I can maintain the long 330 position throughout the period as a hedge for whatever short position or positions I decide to take.

Another form of rolling consists of closing out the profitable short position and rewriting it closer to the money. For example: when the OEX is at $300, I write the 310 CALLS, buy the 315 CALLS, write the 290 PUTS and buy the 285 PUTS. I collect a net premium of $2,000 and have a risk of loss of $5,000 less the premium received i.e., $3,000 maximum loss.

Now the OEX moves to $305. The PUT spread declines in value. I can now close out the spread, or - if I so elect - buy back only the short position of the PUT spread, the 290's - and write the 295's. I have rolled up the PUT spread, and taken a profit on the 290's. My new risk is different than my original risk: my original risk was five points in either direction out-of-the-money. My new risk is ten point in the PUT and five points in the CALL, but I now have more premium in hand and less time before expiration.

Rolling the profitable side of a box spread is often coupled with also rolling the loss side. The combination of the new premium on the profit side and the new premium on the loss side can be a strong mitigating factor controlling potential losses or maintaining an initial profit. For example, in the box spread described above, at the same time I roll up the PUT spread to the 295's, I roll up the CALL spread by buying back the 310 CALLS, selling the original 315 CALLS I purchased, selling more 315 CALLS to develop a short position and buying the 320 CALLS. The result is a new CALL spread at 315 short vs. 320 long. In effect I've moved the box parallel with the market. Commissions become a major factor in these determinations.

E. Hedging A Position

Another way to control or mitigate losses is to hedge the position after it has been placed. The hedging can be used either to lock in a profit or to prevent a further loss. There are generally three ways of hedging a position:

1. Buying stock;
2. Buying an option;
3. Selling an option or a spread.

There is a very wide range of examples which could illustrate the use of these techniques in various situation. I'm not devoting a lot of space to the subject because many hedging strategies are really ways to hold on to profits, not "How to Make Money in Options," which is what this book is about. Once you master the basics presented here, there is plenty of time to read more about the many ways to lock in profits. For illustrative purposes, I am giving one example of each:

Example 1: Buying stock

On April 1, when Ford is at $50, I sell a CALL spread on Ford Motor Co. By selling ten Ford 55 CALLS and buying ten Ford 60 CALLS with an expiration date of May 20. By April 15, Ford stock has gone to 55 and my short position is at-the-money. Not wanting to risk a loss of $1,000 per point on Ford stock, wanting to retain the net premium received on the spread and having confidence that Ford stock will continue to rise, I buy 1,000 shares of Ford stock. Now for every point that Ford stock goes up until $60 I will make $1,000 of unrealized profit on the stock and lose $1,000 on the spread position. If Ford goes back down below $55 during the option period, I will have an unrealized loss on the stock, but not lose anything on the spread and retain the premium received as a hedge against the cost of the Ford stock.

The worst case is if Ford goes to $60 and I lose $5,000 (less the premium) on the option and immediately after the option expires the stock drops to or below my cost. This is called "being whipsawed."

Example 2: Buying an option

To protect an underlying stock portfolio in a market you think will decline, you can buy PUTS. You can buy them

FIGURE V-2 Selling an Option to Hedge a Loss.

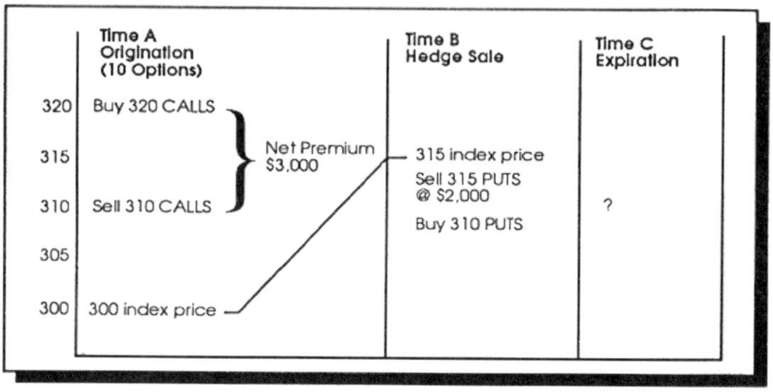

Time A. The potential loss at the origination of the position is $7,000 ($10,000 for the 10 points between 310 and 320 less $3,000 collected in premium. The investor was willing to risk $7,000 for a $3,000 premium because the CALL spread, when put on, was substantially Out-of-the-Money.

Time B. When the index goes to 315, the short position goes "In-the-Money" 5 points, creating a loss of $5,000 in intrinsic value, plus something for Time Value Premium. The amount of Time Value Premium loss should normally be substantially offset by the increase in Time Value Premium of the long position (the 320 CALLS), and, of course, is offset by the new premium.

At this time, the investor sells a PUT spread to hedge. Perhaps a 2 point premium can be received since the short PUT is "At-the-Money" and the market is volatile and bullish. The receipt of $2,000 in premium helps to hedge the potential loss.

Time C. If the market stays at 315 until expiration, the $2,000 premium reduces the loss. If the market goes down, until 310 the investor reduces the loss by $1,000 per point, but suffers a new loss of the same amount on the PUT. If the market continues to rise (which is what is being hedged against) there is the potential for $5,000 of loss, but the total loss risk has been reduced from $7,000 to $5,000.

Two variations are possible, depending on the premium levels and the investor's prediction of the market: (1) The hedge could be a PUT that is "Out-of-the-Money", such as, here, the 310 PUT could be sold, and the 305 bought. This produces a smaller premium but allows for less of a "locked-in" loss if the market reverses and goes down. (2) Alternatively, one could sell an "In-the-Money" PUT — here the 320 — and collect an additional $5,000 of intrinsic premium. The sale of the "In-the-Money" PUT (the 320) is a powerful way to recap the potential loss if the market continues to rise, but it is not profitable if the market stabilizes at 315.

on specific stocks, or - if you have a broadly based port-folio, you can buy those index PUTS which most closely follow your stocks.

Many option traders, when buying PUTS to hedge, will simultaneously sell an out-of-the-money CALL. The pre-mium from the CALL offsets some part of the PUT cost and the positions are consistent (bearish).

Example 3: Selling an option to hedge a deteriorating spread.

On April 2, with the OEX at $305, I put on an OEX CALL spread by selling the May 310 CALLS and buying the 320's. I collect $300 net premium per option. I do 10 con-tracts at all times.

By May 10 the OEX has moved against me to $315. (See Figure V-2.) Now my financial position is as follows:

1. I collected $3,000 in original premium.
2. The 320 CALLS can be sold for $1,000.
3. The 310 CALLS will cost me $7,000 to buy back.
4. My net position at this time is therefore negative $3,000.
    The potential loss of the original position is $10,000 less the $3,000 premium received or $7,000.

With the index at $315, the short position is "in-the-money" 5 points, creating a loss of $5,000 in intrinsic value.

I then sell a PUT spread hedge, by selling the 315 PUT and buying the 310 PUT. Perhaps a $3,000 premium can be obtained to help hedge the potential loss.

Here are the possible results at expiration:

1. If the OEX goes above $320 I will lose $10,000 on the CALL spread, less the $6,000 in total premium collected, for a net loss of $4,000. The PUT spread saved me $3,000 in a fast rising market in which I otherwise would have had a $7,000 loss.

2. When the OEX is between $315 and $320 I will lose $5,000 at $315 and $10,000 at $320 on the CALL spread less the $6,000 premium received for a net of:

320 - $4,000
319 - $3,000
318 - $2,000
317 - $1,000
316    $0
315 + $1,000

3. If the OEX is between $310 and $315 I will lose between $0 (at $315) and $5,000 (at $310) on the PUT spread and lose between $5,000 (at $315) and $0 (at $310) on the CALL spread or a net loss of $5,000 on the box. The $6,000 premium received would then result in a net profit of $1,000.

4. When the OEX falls below $310 I will lose $5,000 on the new PUI spread and gain $6,000 in total premlum collected for a net of $1,000 profit.

Mitigating strategies can become very complex, but they are an essential part of option writing. The key is to take time to work them out and to plan them out - to some degree - in advance of the market move. This is not so difficult to do when the hedging is part of the overall strategy from the beginning - such as buying a PUT at the same time as buying stock, or selling stock in a portfolio and buying CALLS to replace it (neither of which strategies I particularly recommend).

What is difficult is to be prepared for contingencies. Have some ideas of what to do in the event of change when you first put on the position.

Part VI - Tax Considerations

The taxation of options is very complex and goes beyond the scope of this book. As a practical matter, almost all of the past tax deferral advantages to options have been eliminated and the option investor should expect to pay income tax at his customary rate on any gains and generally only offset losses over $3,000 against any other capital gains (in the current year or in the future).

Many option writers take losses on year end positions to offset other gains. In doing so, be careful to avoid the wash sale rule. Methods of hedging during such a 30 day period without running afoul of the wash sale rule are complex, as the tax laws, regulations and interpretations so often vary. When problem arises, you should talk to your accountant.

One important point to remember arises in writing CALLS against a portfolio with a low cost basis. Unlike the buy-write situation, if low basis stock is called away it can create a serious and unexpected tax bill, even if the trades were profitable. The investor, broker or advisor must be very sensitive to this issue when writing CALLS against low basis stocks and the broker or advisor should be sure to fully advise the customer of this additional risk and should work with the customer's accountant to reduce any adverse impact.

PART VII - Lessons to be Learned

A. Three Keys to Keeping Brokers Out of Trouble

In the world of option trading the keys for brokers to use to keep out of trouble are:

1. Proper customer selection;

2. Following a consistent strategy.

3. Adequate communication of the strategy, the risk, and the potential dollar loss to the client.

1. Customer Selection

There are at least three questions to ask yourself before you agree to deal in options for a client:

A. Is it the client's money? If the client is acting as a fiduciary for another, for example, as a family trustee, or for a pension plan - different laws and rules apply. As a general matter I would never write even covered CALLS for a fiduciary without clear evidence - the best is a legal opinion from the customer's lawyer - that option trading is legally permitted for that trust. I would be very wary of doing option strategies not labeled "conservative" strategies" in this book for such a client, irrespective of the trust instrument, with the possible exception of a trustee who is an experienced professional option trader.

B. Can the client bear the loss of the worst case risk? Many clients use the options market as an outlet for gambling instinct. In some ways, this is a socially desirable outlet which may be better than alternatives that offer less chance and may be illegal. Like gambling in general, there can be appropriate situations - a game of gin rummy at the club for ten cents a point - and inappropriate ones - taking the family savings to Las Vegas. Allowing clients to risk the family homestead in the option market is no different. Therefore, thoroughly discuss the client's financial position and discretionary capital and don't be afraid to say no to an order that you believe puts the client at a greater risk than is appropriate for the client's financial position. And don't forget to tell the client when you disagree with a trade, and then mark the confirm "unsolicited." In the long run the client will have more respect for you and believe in your integrity.

C. Does the client know what he or she is doing? This seems to me to be the weakest area for brokers.

Because the truth is, many non-professionals in the options market don't really understand it and are relying on the broker. In these situations, the broker is really taking discretion without acknowledging it and without obtaining the proper forms and approvals.

If your client really wants to trade in options and is in a financial position to do so, consider the following;

a. Don't rely on the client reading the prospectuses sent, or the C.B.O.E. pamphlet on options. It's a fact of life that very few clients ever look at this stuff.

b. It is not enough for the client to just say "yes" to each of your suggestions and acknowledge when the trade is complete. If there is a loss the client did not expect, the chances are he or she will sue.

c. I strongly suggest the following: First, bring an unsophisticated customer into the office and have the customer sit with you while you make a few trades. This converts the experience from one of just words to actually doing it.

Second, with appropriate manager approval, send a letter to the customer confirming the option strategies to be followed and delineating the dollar risks. (See Figures VI-1 and VI-2 for examples of such letters.) One advantage to sending the customer a letter confirming a strategy to be followed is that it forces the broker to follow that

Figure VII-1 Sample Letter to Covered Out-of-the-money
CALL Writing Client.

Dear Sam:

This will confirm our plan to begin writing covered calls against your portfolio in an attempt to generate additional current income.

Since you currently hold 1,000 shares each of IBM, Ford and GM, we will be writing 10 CALLs of various time periods against each of these positions. In general we will try to find CALLs with strike prices that are between 5% and 15% above the current prices of the stock.

As I explained to you, if the stock against which CALLs have been written goes up to or over the strike price, the stock may be bought from you at the strike price. You should check with your tax advisor to see if it is a good (or bad) idea to sell any of these stocks. The sale can be avoided by either buying back the options, or covering the CALL by purchasing new stock at the market price, to deliver to the buyer.

Note that when this happens significantly more commissions result. Also bear in mind that if the stock goes up dramatically, it can be very expensive to do this.

For example, your IBM stock is now $115. We can get two points for the June 125 CALLs, which will net you approximately $1,940 after commissions. If IBM stock goes to $159 in the next 60 days (and it has been there before!), it would cost well over $25,000 to buy back the option, and over $150,000 to buy the 1000 shares of stock needed to meet the call and retain your original holdings.

Please call me if this is in any way not clear, and feel free to come into the office and watch some trading if you want to learn more about the option market.

Sincerely,   *Cecilia*

Figure VII-2 Sample Letter to Uncovered Writing Client.

Dear Mr. Smythe, Jr.:

This will confirm that we have now begun writing uncovered combinations in your account.

As I understand the strategy you are following, you are writing an out-of-the-money CALL and an out-of-the-money PUT on certain stocks which you follow. Your strategy is to write far enough out-of-the-money to capture the two premiums when the stock volatility maintains the stock price between your parameters, and to hedge or roll when either side gets in-the-money.

As you know, writing these combinations subjects you to very high risk of loss if the market is strongly volatile in either direction. For example, in Oct. 1987, the market dropped over 500 points in a few days, the option market was non-liquid, and PUT option prices soared. Under such circumstances, a short combination such as you recently wrote, with 25 contracts on each side, could lose well over $1 million in a 500 point drop.

While your financial position, as set forth in your Jan. 1988 statement, reflects enough net worth to sustain such a loss, I do want to suggest that you consider buying a hedge position on each side to limit the potential losses from your positions.

Please feel free to call me or come into the office if you wish to explore this in greater depth.

Sincerely,

Ambrose

strategy or the broker may face serious criticism.

Finally, do not depend on your compliance staff; check yourself to see that the client has executed the proper option trading forms, that the strategies in use are on the forms - specifically - and that the financial data is current. If the financial data is not current, send a letter asking for an update if there has been a change.

2. Following A Consistent Strategy

Sometimes brokers act in an inconsistent way out of ignorance. But more often they try to recoup losses, to maintain the customer, by taking greater risk. It is not uncommon to see an out-of-the-money option writer suddenly begin to write deep in the money options to generate cash in an account that has sustained major losses. This change of strategy - eliminating the "window of profit" - is usually not justified and puts the client at greater risk than the original strategy.

Sometimes one sees the converse - a successful, profitable strategy that goes to the broker's head, so the broker becomes more aggressive - for example, the broker may change from writing CALL spreads to writing uncovered CALLS.

The safest way to protect yourself against criticism is to clearly define your strategies (i.e., covered CALL writing out-of-the-money, letting stock be called away) and stick to them. Accept losses and reach an agreement on new or changed strategies when appropriate, then confirm the changes by letter.

3. Adequate Communication Of Strategy And Method

How much needs to be communicated and how much confirmed in writing? Not too much. As long as the communication meets three tests:
1. Name the strategy;
2. Leave open the door for more information;
3. State - in dollars - the risk level, where appropriate.

In my opinion, the use of letters of this type would eliminate much of the conflict and litigation that exist in option trading and I do not understand why brokers and brokerage firms do not begin to use them on a regular basis.

B. Lessons For Lawyers

In large part, the lessons to be learned for lawyers derive from the suggestions made to brokers - were these recommendations followed or not? Unfortunately, the way lawyers traditionally look at stock market cases is often not appropriate. For example, in stock cases one compares the investment with the commissions generated, or one looks at "turnover," the ratio of sales to holdings. These are not very good indices of improper options trading. In trading options, one expects greater commissions; the box spread above consists of four options for each combination put on. Because of the limited life of options, by definition there is more turnover.

The lawyer handling option controversies and trying to analyze what went wrong is often burdened by having a client. The claimant may exaggerate his or her lack of information about the strategies and the trades. The broker may try to hide the degree of control exercised by the broker over the decision making and often fails to volunteer the real reasons behind certain strategies. For example, out-of-the-money option writers sometimes switch to deep in-the-money writing to generate larger cash balances. And one sometimes sees a steady increase in the number of options bought or sold, as losses are incurred - a familiar form of "doubling up" as it is called in Las Vegas. This may be appropriate if disclosed to the client, but is sometimes used to cover-up losses. There may be an inappropriate change to a higher risk strategy.

The approach I recommend for lawyers is to identify the strategy or strategies employed and to determine the answers to the following questions:

a. Were they consistently followed?

b. Were they appropriate for this client?

c. Were they communicated to the client?

d. Did the client understand?

e. Even if the strategies were communicated, was the degree of risk and the potential dollar loss communicated and understood?

f. Did the client correctly disclose to the broker the client's true financial position and willingness and ability to accept losses?

g. What level of participation did the client have in the extent and level of trading and the acceptance of risk?

In many cases, pursuing the answers to these questions leads one to the conclusion that some blame for the losses falls on both sides to the controversy. Thus, it is not uncommon for courts, juries and arbitrators to reach compromise decisions. Often both sides are unhappy with such decisions because both sides come out with financial losses in such cases, particularly after payment of attorney's fees. It is, therefore, important for the lawyer handling such cases to communicate to the client those facts which the lawyer discovers which point to fault by the lawyer's client, so that the client does not have unrealistic expectations.

A recurring theme in options controversies boils down to a question of timing. Learning is a process and clients often learn about options during the process of watching the trades suggested by the broker. When a loss occurs in the middle of such a process, the question that arises is where the client was in the learning process.

In one famous court case, the court was faced with such a situation. The essence of the court's holding was that the customer was inexperienced during the first year of trading and thus the broker was responsible for losses during that period. But after a year of trading the customer was sufficiently knowledgeable to evaluate the risk himself. Thus, losses in year two were not recoverable.

I once handled a case with a variation on this theme. The client put himself in the hands of a broker who made inappropriate trades, some of which were made while the client was out of the country. When the client returned and discovered extensive losses and trades, he angrily accused the broker of fraud and deception. The broker admitted his errors and begged for another chance to make up the losses. The client agreed, thinking that the broker was so afraid of disclosure that he would see that profits were generated. Further losses resulted. The arbitrators in this matter awarded reimbursement of the losses before discovery, but not those arising afterward. This seems consistent with the court's decision in the case above.

Using Professional Witnesses

A group of expert witnesses has evolved who testify in option cases. Naturally, these witnesses, the lawyers from the firms handling the bulk of the cases - (usually the defense side), and the arbitrators all know each other. Needless to say, this doesn't hurt the defense of these cases.

In complex cases, these experts can be extremely helpful - perhaps indispensable. Even with such experts available, a lawyer knowledgeable about options is a major asset in options cases, because the expert testimony involving judgment is often skewed and biased.

For example:

Beware of exaggeration by the claimant's expert. In writing a naked CALL, the risk is theoretically infinite. The expert can, therefore, claim that hundreds of thousands of dollars were at risk, which is a larger risk than a claimant with his particular net worth should bear. While the conclusion may be correct, the dollar figure is often exaggerated. The upside of a particular stock in a 30-day period can be historically and statistically evaluated and is not really infinite.

By the same token, if IBM stock is at $100, and a 100 PUT is written, while the theoretical loss is 100 points, as a practical matter it is virtually impossible for IBM stock to go to zero. Even companies that go into bankruptcy normally retain some stock value. Furthermore, remember that the brokerage house will typically sell out a customer when the loss reaches a certain point, if the customer has not covered the new margin requirement. So this is typically the point at which the maximum loss can be quantified. For example, a customer with $10,000 in equity might be sold out if the stock dropped from $100 to $90 and therefore really only has a downside risk potential of $10,000, not $100,000.

On the defense side, this fact can be taken advantage of by explaining that while there was no downside hedge position written, as a practical matter there is a stop loss near the margin requirement, so the customer is protected to that extent. This is generally true, although in a few cases the market has dropped too fast for the broker to sell out the client at the desired level.

One should also be aware of expert testimony which is theoretically correct, but not of substantive value to the case in point.

For example, naked writing on the OEX is arguably less risky than naked writing on specific stocks. This is because in writing, say, a PUT against a stock like IBM, there is always the possibility of unusual and specific news about IBM causing a sudden and unexpected decline in the stock. This can be news as innocuous as reduced earnings, or as serious as the massive fraud that was discovered at Equity Funding Corporation, or Technical Equities. But, in writing against the OEX, these "blips" are virtually eliminated. Even if sudden unexpected information is discovered about one company that makes up a part of the index, it will not have that much of an effect on the overall index. There is, therefore, less risk in writing on the OEX than in writing against specific stocks. From this point of view, it can be honestly said that writing naked options on the OEX has a certain conservative nature to it, but this is more of a theoretical difference than one of substance.

Because options controversies arise out of an agreement between the customer and the brokerage house, that agreement should be the starting point for the lawyer. Jurisdictions differ in a number of legal rules involving these controversies, but in general, customer agreements usually provide that option controversies (not involving commodities) are subject to mandatory arbitration before either the NASD (National Association of Securities Dealers) for the NYSE (New York Stock Exchange), at he client's election. Each of these bodies publishes books explaining their procedures and setting forth their rules, which should be carefully reviewed.

PART VIII - Conclusion

Options can be an interesting and profitable investment. They can provide a source of income. They can
also be used to protect other investments. Because of
their limited life and the complexity of many option strategies, they require more knowledge and more attention
than other stock market investments. Option writing is not
for the faint of heart, or those who cannot psychologically
accept losses from time-to-time.

Many option investors lose money in unexpected
amounts because they fail to understand the basic difference between buying something and selling first with a
potential obligation to buy back later. They fail to assimi-
late the potential for ending up with a debit balance,
requiring the payment of more funds than originally
required (unlike the purchase situation).

Option BUYERS usually lose money. By the nature of
the market and premium prices only the clairvoyant seem
to profit from the pure purchase of an option.

The use of high risk, or open-ended loss potential

strategies is only appropriate for a limited number of investors and should be avoided except where many factors are confirmed and well communicated.

The use of inconsistent strategies, strategies inappropriate to the investor, or strategies not fully understood by both the investor and the broker should be avoided. In the case of controversies, inconsistent and inappropriate strategies can result in liability to the broker.

In spite of the many who lose, there are a number of conservative option strategies, not well known to non-professional investors, that offer a statistically reasonable likelihood of profit within the confines of defined dollar risk.